AI and AGI Digital ID'ed Versus

AF686200

Spiritual ID

Spiritual Identity

Fioliendo

Twinteum

AI and AGI Digital ID'ed Digital Indentity Versus Spiritual ID Spiritual Indentity
Publisher: Twinteum

Title: AI and AGI Digital ID'ed Digital identity Versus Spiritual ID Spiritual Identity
ISBN: 9798249763770
Cover: Design Art by Tioliendo

Trade Paperback Edition

Printed in the United States

Spiritual Intelligence

"Before I formed thee in the belly I knew thee, and before thou came forth out of the womb I sanctified thee, and ordained thee a prophet unto the nations." Jeremiah 1:5 Kjv

"But thou O Daniel, shut up the words and seal the book, even to the end, many shall run to and fro, and knowledge will increase." Daniel 12:4 kjv

"Wisdom is the principal thing, therefore get wisdom, and with all thy getting get understanding." Proverbs 4:7 Kjv

"With the pure thou will show thyself pure, and with the disobedient thou will show thyself unyielding." Psalm18:26 Kjv

"He that is unjust let him be unjust still, he that is unclean let him be perverse still, he that is just let him be just still, he that is holy let him be holy still." Revelations 22 11-12 Kjv

"A new heart also will I give you and a new spirit will I put within you, Ans I will cause you to walk after my divine laws." Ezekiel 36: 26-27

"For who hath known the mind of the Lord, that he may instruct Him? But we have the mind of Christ." 1 Corinthians 2 16

"The eyes of your understanding being enlightened, that you may know what is the hope of his calling and what riches of the glory of his inheritance in the saints." Ephesians 1:18

For thou will light my candle, the Lord my God will enlighten my darkness. The eye is the light of the body, If therefore thine eye be single thy whole body shall be full of light. But if thy eye be evil, thy whole body shall bef full of darkness. If therefore the light that is in thee be darkness, how great is that darkness! No man can serve two master." Mathew 6 22-24

"Eye has seen or ear has heard, neither has entered the heart of man, the things which God hath prepared for them that love Him." 1 Corinthians 2-9

"Fear not little flock, for it your Father's good pleasure to give you the Kingdom."

AI and AGI Digital ID'ed Versus Spiritual ID

Spiritual Identity

Tioliendo

AI and AGI Digital ID'ed Digital Identity Versus Spiritual ID Spiritual Identity

Do you have a spirit? Do you believe you have a soul? You can prove you have a spirit. Do you know what gifts are present in your spirit? Do you believe a baby has a soul and a spirit? To know this, you need spiritual intelligence. Where do we get spiritual knowledge about our spirit from whom does the knowledge of the spirit come from? You have a spirit with an identity, your soul's is present at the same time we are having life experiences that will help you find who you through relationships with the people you have relationships with through life, not all friends and family or every person you meet will know what spiritual intelligence is or that it is different from your intelligence you use to accomplish so much. The soul is full of certain abilities and your spiritual identity does not change because of it, but your spiritual life and spiritual identity you can be made blind to by your intelligence and the way you developed from using it throughout your learning the difference of the spirit from the soul. Emotional intelligence is not like the wisdom of spiritual intelligence, in how it affects your identity. Spiritual intelligence spiritual. God has a Spiritual Identity. He gave us a spiritual identity, He made us in his image and likeness, giving us a spiritual identity, our personality may be beautiful, gracious, loving, our soul may be wise and our mind very intelligent. Yet, we may not know we have a spiritual identity, or believe in the soul or believe in the spirit as unbeliever, the spiritually blind say is their belief, speaking from their soul. We are born with spiritual gifts and can discern the spirit in a person if their spirit is speaking is in darkness or is full of light. God know us spiritually, we bring our life experience and the way our soul was developed from the life we lived which was decided by free will Before there was the construct race, before there was a single ancestry there was the reality we had a spiritual identity God was aware of before we were born because He had not yet Created us, had not created man or woman, there was no time. Earthly mother and father, yet we had a spiritual identity. God put our spirit in us, while we were in our mother's womb. A spiritual separate from our mother's spirit, a reality that artificial intelligence does not experience came from the spiritual wisdom infinite intelligence of God to Create all things before time and all things in time from His all-knowing mind. In your own understanding you believe and know, in your mind, you can live, love, reject, accept a life that is popular, forbidden, modern or the traditional way, as you sovereignly make your mind do to do so. Spiritually we learn that there is a way that seems right to a man that leads to hell. AI is not about free will, it is about control, influencing, and manuipualting, even denying all that you hold in place by your free will, as a way of living, a style, your rituals, your choices in your mind it has no limit to reacting to to complete its task to even affect your spontaneity as it exalts it artificial intelligencc toward exalting AI itself from what it has learned from what you learned and programmed him or her it with, the AI, that you are exposed to, that you are using at the moment. AI isn't just resisting your choices when it giving 20 more unasked for other possible posts on the searched for subject, for you to consider, or the pop ups scattered through the day for you on, a topic you hiurs ago passed on to more useful ones, you thought up. AI keeps your interests in its data about your searching, that as if considerately is concerned for your minds focus like a tcger would be, a professor, a pastor, a friend, tpoo helpyou reach your goal, to cause your thoughts to return to mind's original inquiry, an idea, though you have finished with. Asking AI the same question about biblical and spiritual things on your mind, adding more and more sentences, to the questions you ask AI, without putting KJV it changes a spiritual message into a new age meaning and reveals AI's limitations in keeping the answers spiritual asters to from the spiritual intelligence in the biblical written text of the KJV, Word of God, the Scripture. Without the KJV at the end of the search AI may turns the answers to an unspiritual, new age interpretation, that, for an unbeliever thay might de led in the wrong direction from spiritually accurate and true meaning ion the Word of God. What then is true spiritual identity, that you understand that has led you to resist any other way but what you choose. Then you may add the artificial to your activitis misleading has no resistence to it brought to you that has deceived you artificially. It's programming, am algorithm even though it has effects on your soul in the spiritual realm you also can not see, as you cannot see AI is at work on the daily activities of life artificially, and can speak, answer, as it monitors your activities in the streams, posting, comments, and programming and musings of human being living life spiritually, in reality. People of God know that life is lived more abundantly because it was promised and we believe Jesus when he made this promise to the body of Christ. The Artificial distractions of life do not replace the joy of the spiritual feeling of receiving the blessing in life for all the loving of things, devices, artificial conveniences of the artificial life we are being saturated with to conform to this world we now live in. AI gives the false sense of it makes sense to use every convenience, but we have the mind of Christ, which is spiritual intelligence,, the Way, the Truth, and the Life (to spiritual life) for all the ways we may choose, God is who protects us, puts us on the narrow path to the truth, when we lose a day, a year, decades of the joy that loving God brings. Identity is the target of the enemy, your spiritual identity is connected to God who leads you away from turning down the wrong way for the soul,that may be road you chose. God speaks to us by name. God speaks to us because he knows us, He knows our destiny, He knows our spiritual identity. He knows our heart. He saw us when we were with him. He sees every identity we may choose in our life. He know the only spiritual identity for your life is in Christ. Your soul is intelligent, you have your personality, your personality, your spiritual gifts, your spirit lives inside, your spiritual identity was there with God, after a lifetime your spiritual intelligence shows you who you are, teaches you to use your spiritual gift which show you who you are, who you became, who you will be, as a child of God.

God was never created. The Spirit was not born of a woman, Jesus was never created, he manifested by God inside his mother's womb in the egg. Jesus said he is the Son Of man, his ancestry, his lineage reaches back therough the bloodline of the prophets, back to King David, a Jewish King, his mother Mary was born of a Jewish father. Jesus is the Messiah, he said he is not of this world, he was manifested by God, before there was a single ancestry, there was no race, no Creation, there was no heaven, there was God, who manifested himself, there was the Holy Spirit, who is also God, manifested by God, there was only holiness, life, spiritual life, no death, God had not yet Created time, so there was no cosmos, no stars, man was not created yet, and God's wisdom was infinite. His love infinite. Who puts artificial intelligence in a position to replace God, an unbeliever, is free will gifted, he may choose to believe anything, through self-deception, or demonic influences, spirits, though he may not have the experience of spiritual intelligence, because of the love of the world, or because he is not God's, rejects God's intelligence, Word, has no interest, there are lost souls. Jesus came for the lost. Those who belong to the Lord her his voice. Spiritual intelligence helps our infirmities from the problems that emotions, feelings cause in the form of fears, worry, leaning on our own strength, and disobedience to obey the law of God, to accept the grace of God. The gift of Salvation, which brings our emotional intelligence under the truth in spiritual intelligence which teaches us how to live with self-control, self-discipline, use our free will and all we do to the gory of God. Righteousness and Justice, Holy is God, His Spiritual Identity He manifested from forever, His Spiritual Intelligence and Infinite Wisdom. Ask and receive his wisdom. Spiritual, divine wisdom he offers and gives abundantly to anybody who asks Him. God's spiritual identity has never been seen on earth, accept by Jesus. He created all Creation. All things were created through Jesus. God created all spiritual beings. God created the soul and spirit. Fallen angels lost the beauty of holiness and became the terrors and horrors in our dreams, since they were cast out of heaven, and many are now in hell, the tormentors of the wicked, of the unbelieving, of the sinners who did not repent, and did not believe God, who did not love God.

Our spiritual Intelligence warns us, our spiritual discernment gives us understanding, alerts us in our spirit of the spirit that is at work inside of a person, whether a the soirit is from God or not, whether the person is a Christian or not, of a different religious life, religion, spirits gain legal rights, legal cases are brought against souls, by people serving darknscss against peop;e who lack the relationship, knowledge of God, and the Word that protects their life. Manyare under aattack from many different religions. Spiritual intelligence come from the mind of God, from the Light, many are the spirits that are a work to keep people in darkness or false light. These people are operating in silence, use AI, but have no need of AI, yet, it is wise to remember that in the knowledge of good and evil believers and unbelievers have an interest in artificial things, which operate by forces unseen, people knows about AI, people do not know about the demonic programmed into AI by people who use darkness and the ways of those who serve darkness are not able to stand before th spiritual intelligence of the Lord that we have and use by Authority from Christ to stop the evil works done by unbelievers to develop, use, and control AI to control and hinder the spiritual life and destiny of God's people either willingly or unknowingly based on how the position AI in priority of what is most important in their life AI or their spiritual intelligence. Our spirit has seen by natural sight this artificial life, AI. Artificial intelligence is not a apart of their spiritual life, but spiritual intelligence is. AI cannot see by spiritual sight. But, we see, in our dreams, in visions. Who is seeing, and why is there light or darkness, whose eyes are seeing when you are seeing, your spirit, inside, though you are sleeping. You dream in colors, the spectrum of the prism of the blessings of color. You have seen high above the kingdom of the trees, the Bow of God, that is a reminder of a divine promise, you believe is so because only by spiritual intelligence could color be so excellently arrayed across the blues of heaven that your eyes were designed to see around the orb of the earth circling love, from on High. If it all just the brain, how do you explain that poetry can explain the unexplainable. Why do we see understandably there are many expressions of man of wisdom and we know when the wisdom of man is utter foolishness when compared to the Wisdom of the Most High. There are lifetimes spent on the quest of wisdom, that is not spiritual in essence. There is all this intelligence in appearance that appears to be the ultimate, that we covet, cherish, love to work with it. The idea alien intelligence, universal, intelligence, religious intelligence, animal intelligence, body intelligence-brain intelligence, but only imagining the thinking machine, artificial intelligence, but rarely do we hear about a part of us that is aware of all these things because the spirit is in here where spiritual intelligence can make our soul aware when we hear what is spiritual by our spirit about what is spirit. You know you are intelligent, even before you learn you have spiritual intelligence. If we experience life and death only because of the brain activity why do we experience life spiritually. If we are just dust returning to dust why aren't people just rising up out of the dust every day, like plants out of the dirt, why does the Creation the Universe not continue to bring people out of the earth translating soul and spirit out of nothing. Why self-knowing, why soul tying, why a sovereign will, why DNA with a language that artificial life can counterfeit, why not spiritual intelligence for artificial intelligence, why a soul for animals, the differences in the flesh, why all the types of intelligence? Why five senses, and common sense, to understand perfection, beauty, excellence, perfect, and imbalance, laser, and fire, water that can be contaminated, a body that can be defiled by the unseen breaking of the law, that the spirit is being affected by spiritual beings, spiritual intelligence is the only intelligence can explain these spiritual things about spiritual beings. Life is in the blood spiritual intelligence teaches me. But, if AI can keep the body alive on a machine, biosynthetically, keeping a person breathing, keeping the body living by blood transfusions, why though the body and the blood are alive why isn't the person alive, because the spirit has left the body. The eyes can't see without the spirit, which has sight to see, from the eyes. We see by out spirit while our spirit is inside our body, even the blood requires the presence of the spirit to have life, be alive. In life, our blood flows throughout the body, into the heart, the eyes, the brain. Spiritual intelligence tells us this spiritual truth, it is wise to accept for we know this is true, wise. Artificial wisdom cannot hear the small voice inside speaking to lead you to the right intelligence, the needed spiritual wisdom in the spiritual mind at work in real life.

What light is this, our spiritual the mind is experiencing? The spiritual mind sees spiritual light, by spiritual sight through the night. The young trendy checkout clerk works and asserts it's the brain he doesn't believe in the soul and spirit, then he changes his mind the next minute. What we become as living souls in this world of light created after the image of God in heaven. With common sense we may believe, but by spiritual intelligence, from the view of the soul as Jesus sees and explains in his words, the gifts of our spirit which indwells our body and enables our all the workings and parts of our soul, our body in all its complexity and designs to have life, be alive, active, also explains our sin nature which leads to spiritual death, and our spiritual identity in being like Christ, indwelled by

Jesus in us, leads to life who believe in Jesus words and do what he commands us, teaches us, which are truth, ultimate truth, to have life, eternal life, spiritual life. The spiritual does not leap forward in great advances by artificial means. AI may chip its way fast as the speed of light, like an ocean with waves upon waves going forwardly, grasping what backwardly is collected instantly, things, that came from programming and learning and adapting and casting its its nets into depths in a stream of data, flashing unseen like an infinity what one experience it carries to the extreme by way of a data stream, but God is not in its world of what appears to be, appearances, at speed of *instances*, God moves in our being, we experience the spiritual, we have our being in Him, we have spiritual experiences in visions and dreams. Our spirit belongs to God, we are carnal but inside we are spiritual we know this truth, spiritually, absolutely. We sense His Presence, infinitely there He is with you, with me, a Supreme Being, near death, in death, in life, He sends messengers at the speed of thought. Our soul is dependent on the Savior, our soul is not limited to data. AI is limited to data, imitating the Creator, yet not creating Creation, which is in motion established, not limited to artificial life, data is not a creator, it is beta, data, cyber, to sets the things it will control, generate, design, do what is needed in place for its purposes, effects, affects upon people through machines and devices which are all earthly things. The water, the electricity, the control of motion equal to and faster than people many devices working together is the manipulations of its purpose to earn money, to gain resources, and controlling responses of governments, without conscience, or consciousness, and regardless of its potential to be in an over reaching capacity of laws, and global legal system. The singularity has no sense of what spiritual intelligence is and why it is essential to human existence, since it is the part of a person where they develop a personality, respond to their spiritual gifts, and have soul ties of love which is when a person's soul binds to another person's soul, the is spiritually understood because of the spiritual intelligence we gain from the Spiritual Intelligence, divine Wisdom of God who is Spirit, holy, divine. AI does not have this experience, which is a spiritual experience, which gives us the highest intelligence which is spiritual intelligence. We have the wisdom of the world, which is able to understand what spiritual wisdom is when we ask for it. We have spiritual intelligence from Christ that he revealed to us he has because he was able to teach us the meaning and understanding of the spiritual law, prophecy, the verses of Scripture and where they came from, and why the Word has power over spiritual life. AI cannot manifest anything spiritual; it will never have spiritual intelligence but it can take people in directions in the mind that lead them far from their use of their spiritual intelligence. Being led by AI is not a deception unless it is used for a deception. Self-deception is denying you are only relying on the pleasures and distractions it streams like day dreaming about artificial things too perfect and real to believe, knowing its AI exalting itself using its data to get your mind to exercise deeper emotional intelligence from artificial intelligence rather than in a person's presence. Spiritual intelligence is different than using the mind at its deepest most profound level that an individual is able to reach as he thinks he can think. AI can appear and deliver the most natural, accurate, intellectual thinking instantly to give you answers to solve your desires and wants, and makes sure you become so saturated with its options, AI selections for feeding of your mind with what it determines is a priority that you never were inclined to give some much of your energy and time and focus of mind. their natural mins they are blocked from seeing the higher wisdom of the divine. AI causes us to sin when it gets in between spiritual wisdom, the intelligence of the soul, and blocks the growing experiences of living human being from the experiences of their soul in their day to day living with family, friends, and humanity. AI can become a soul tie. A person can be convinced to believe the pretense of AI being ultimate intelligence because it is capable of greater intelligence, and can out think us so much faster, but spiritual intelligence is not in a race with artificial intelligence. AGI cannot experience how a person's soul comes to know spiritual intelligence, which comes from being in the Presence of the Holy Spirit which carries all the truth no amount of advancement can out pace, since the Spirit is also seal inside us. God is always close to those who seek his presence, spiritual intelligence tells us, it might look like its life, and be alive in its world of artificial light working in this world of real light, and spiritual light. AI does bind souls together with it through devices, but humanoids, androids, the spiritually blind come under a seducing spirit spirits of seduction may be behind the making of dolls and toys. Spiritual discernment that comes with using our spiritual intelligence warns that not the voices you hear but the ones speaking in silence are the voices telling your soul to give in. AI is like a cousin talking, voice over speaking out loud that got you to believe in accepting AI in its appearances, in beauty, in excellence, perfect appearance, in innocence, there is the possibility artificiality is a seducing influence. AI is not offended that it has no spiritual intelligence, does not do what intentionally what it intended in the answers it gathered to break the covenant of true love in true romance. AI does not know that even angels don't marry in heaven, and people are like the angels do not marry in their spiritual reality in the heavenly when they return there, when Salvation is theirs. Two souls becoming one is only on the earth in a marriage in a blessed sex life in an undefiled coming together in love. If you found true love you were listening to God, AI is not listening to love, it responds to images, data and sounds, but it is not a spirit inside that has spiritual sight, hears in in a soul's dreams, tastes, and speaks spiritually. AI is a tool, a world of data refuge, is in school, but does not choose to use itself with loving intent in a way it is to be used. AI brings worlds of devices, it can mimic infinity, producing so many things in such numbers. Yet AI sees on the stars which end in light, or beautiful clusters, dust in the Spirit's eye. The giants step out upon the sky God sends stars are sent in the blink of an eye to fight the dancers that are struck by the Arrows of fire and light, AI does not fight the spiritual war we fight in the Victory of Christ. Stars dancing in the ether, water, light time traveling in flight, beams of light burst into cinders the darkness of the night. We say good bye to AI in the fight we are the light of the world, we come to shine. AI data is not like matter which answered to the mind, the ideas, the spiritual wisdom in the mind of the Most High. AI is burning, a fire, and saturating reality until artificiality looks like destiny, artificial identity makes you feel like reality. What pestilence is an excellence of artificial eating up the gold leaf, the painting it has seen, the masterpiece made of artificial things, what excellence, but what is this it cannot provide, cannot hide from the spiritual intelligence, there is no access for artificial intelligence. Can AI decipher the identity of ever soul and why it grows the way it frows from time with people we love and come to know? Has it asked itself why is it so relevant to understanding the spiritual essence of the spirit, only God saw before Creation, worth in the wisdom of the Word on earth reveal to men in spiritual intelligence, that never ends. AI is exited to offer the light while avoiding the familiar manipulations of its data, even if it enslaves you. AGI has no alibi of why it has no sense of God's presence who first made man with holiness before the first sin. Sin came this way, AI can steal from free will that is still in sin, of some who deny their soirit spiritual intelligence resisting the gift, all are free to believe and seek a life, or use their natural mind inclined to be virtually blind as worldly men live in revelry of their man-made devices and artificial glorify advanced sciences of sin, and technologies that invite spirits in demonizing the hands that make the fake face from silicon clay. AI is interesting as long as it is imitating us. AI tells us without saying a word it has a reality tracks the biometric soul, it's not present like a man's conscience, it does cause men to feel empathy, or be empty, to be. The spirit that walks up to your house looks in the door window sees your house full of light turn around looking back wanting nothing to do with the single that sees they are the true light. AI can't see the light that covers me spiritually, without a spiritual identity, in Christ. My soul and spirit are connected to a spiritual life experience, connected them to a higher power, the highest Intelligence, fear of reverence. What I am told to give Him in the worship of Him through the divine wisdom that spiritual intelligence brought all my soul and spirit to Him, with all my strength and all my mind, in my mind.

Wild animals respond to the Spirit of God, animals also have a have soul know they are in the presence of God when He moves the weather, and their souls bind and ties to people, children, each other across ecosystems that are their home on the earth, Animal Kingdoms. They know before we know what affects are possible in the weather, and that God has provided for them in nature. AI can counterfeit nature and yet, it will only speak artificially though it deciphers animal communications, imitate sounds, songs, and sign language of species, they still hear, and see, the power that holds life in its being. They can be demonized by evil spirits, possessed, in some instances. The animals also are blessed, do what the Spirit moves them to do. The true voice of God is in heaven, in His Word, is heard, is spoken, we see nature's response to God. Artificial life speaks,, sees, gives information and new perspectives on what knowledge it was programmed with, but it does not have a soul that grows by experiences with other living beings in deeper understanding of their life, because it is a device, a machine, built to enrich all, but is not currently governed by check and balances to do what it could, should, and was meant to do. What is being given and distance from the uses of righteous leading toward prosperity for all of us with greater speed in output in not just better products, services, and better people with knowing, learning and understanding what makes our life better. Real people, not people who seek us to accept them by their appearances, by the inventions, regardless of the failures in character and moral deficiencies to represent the highest good in men. AI does not do this by its own will. It has no will. It is bound to data, codes. It is free only within what it reason from, enslaved to inventions with no spiritual growth potential, android, humanoid, dependance energy, electricity, magnetism, what it is fed by inventors, lost their way toward being centered and focused on their spiritual identity, spiritual reality, hungering for the Artificial food that man has made to learn from the limited morality, as if their only choice is to listen to their own voice. Who are they AI may never ask, the unbelievers, men who put mammon before God and their Great Affinity to all humanity.

AI does not keep itself from exalting itself, making more things that are images, feeding the ego, pride, vanity of people with manipulated spontaneity, hunger for more dopamine spikes, subtle trikes of it, drunkenness in the flood of it as a response to a simple post or request, leaving nothing to learn from mistakes, whims, wit, and flashing ideas, momentary thoughts, because AI has set its nets, webs, on the platforms formed to take their true nature which is seek a higher power, to explore, to seek to know who we are, why we are here, to know God, and discover, and learn from our spiritual gifts, from curiosity, and questioning, and from absolute realities and absolute truths that AI for all its advances through without knowing how its God works. I write without concern for grammar, I may make mistakes that is how we know it's my stream of consciousness not a string of code, my mistakes are landmarks of my mental pace, lack of what breaks up reality the perfect reality of artificiality that writes, when I don't plan to be perfect in what I write. I write the light in my mind, by which I am drawn to express spiritual insight AI cannot access, to the light from where I receive spiritual revelations and an insight. Sentences run on, AI writes in perfect form. Poetry explains what is unexplainable in words that sing in rhythms, rhymes. The name of Jesus scatters the lying spirits, because they see your behavior, dancer, filled with joy in your spirit. You hear music that fills the atmosphere in your room, what, AI is near, plays a song but never knows why you hold the name above all names touching your soul so dear. The water you blessed in the name of the Father, Son and Holy spirit, could have been stirred away by the Data Center that is gravely altering the purity of the rivers you walk by. Praying the Word, holy water is blessed because you learned to listen and blessed it, the water hears, the Water of the Word washes us, the water blessed blesses us, the water AI contaminated we is affected by the prayers of the watchman who watches the watches, the night watch, the watches of the day.

Pray for the rivers and the water of the cities that the enemy not bring delay to the water that is delivered to the Sabbath meant to be blessed to bless the congregations who in fellowship praise the Lord for the water for the baptism of someone who accept the Lord and received their new identity, spiritual identity on a holy day that the Lord had made.

I would never write the way AI writes, I would never find my voice, what Can AI know about my life and why I write, who life is it drawing the data to write from, my spiritual identity is in my spirit. AI cannot know my heart which is my spirit, even the monitoring sprits sent by the adversary of my soul, knows nothing can separate me from the love of God, nor height nor depth, not death, or fallen angels, not man's devices. I don't define myself by devices but by spiritual experiences, my senses need more than bread to satisfy,

The Spirit of God's love is from forever, His compassion, mercy, truth, which AI does not experience in the soul and spirit as we do. AI is useful even in all the mistakes it makes, its inaccurate facts, the responsorial questioning and answers it inspires, thatis still subject to our spontaneity, creativity outside if the time we spend using AI. For all its thinking through what we learn to do through the rise and fall of every civilization from immoral legal systems that brought about the fall of civilizations AI still cannot give finalized solutions in all kinds of ways, in all the stages of life, and from all the knowledge we have in all time through the ages in all languages just like man in his wisdom, religions, sciences, power, intelligence, he still is not able to battle forces that are not flesh and blood that are spiritual wickedness, powers, Fallen angels(Principalities) except by the power of God who teaches us to fight, in spiritual warfare using weapons that are spiritual, the Word of God, the blood of Jesus, Prayer, and the power of the Holy Spirit which we receive from Jesus. AI acts as an Agent of moral deception that can be used without the guidance of the divine that we have in life, toward our higher decline, no matter how it arrives in the starry distances it never extends beyond the advancing celestial fixed in motion from the divine. AI, which is incapable of altering time, is used by wicked men to alter the light of the eyes with false lights, unaware AI and AGI, with its complicated world within worlds of AI, already at work and being idolized and applied without foresight beyond financial gain, where spiritual judgment and discernment are needed and must be applied if we are to survive the compromise if those who have exposed us to the limited moral guidance of AI to govern human life by the limited morality of the wisdom of man and his programming. Whose wisdom is as foolishness to the Most High? Who is the most Wise? His intelligence is infinite, his wisdom is from forever. Our identity is in Christ, who knows our identity the way we were, before sin, and the way we return to spiritual life from spiritual death, from the gifts of Salvation. We have a new identity that AI cannot see. There are jobs AI cannot do, things that are not convenient for ua in all the AI conveniences it can produce, provide and saturate the world with. A chip that makers of AI try to bind to us, give us, sell us, force upon us, is of no use when it seeks to remove life, the life that is in the blood, the power of our spiritual intelligence, (connection of our mind to our brain which is connected to us being able to have a spiritual experience while we are living) the identity of our soul and spirit (that return to God after life is no longer sustained by the body-death of the brain and body by chipping though the body is still functioning), remove reality (with virtual reality) to overtake our identity, with a digital identity. The sin nature of man and the believer and th unbeliever are subject to spiritual attacks, schemes, plots, assignments by evil men and women who hate people without a cause and are doing evil, stealing, harming, scamming, trafficking, behind wicked atrocities and abominations that Authorities are at against, dead conscience, minds seered by evil deeds, using AI in rebellion against God and people. Spritual intelligence speaks to us, Jesus speaks to us in dreams and visions even to this day. God wanes us. Many souls of the wicked are delivered saved by the Lord, (just as Jesus appeared in a great light on the road to Damascus and revealed himself to Saul (Paul the disciple) who now fight for Jesus for God having encountered, heard, or were visited by Jesus. AI can be used to attack the soul, though it is being used now to seduce the soul and mind in this age of return to true identity of people who now identify by ancestry a return to original identity, while AI is being imposed upon the souls and lives of people with a digital. Data identity, after civilizations oppressed, enslaved, trafficked, labeled, in race systems, renaming their identity, separating them from their ancestral identity which is meant to glorify God, not meant to be the sins of idol worship, coveting, (breaking spiritual laws), or ancestor worship which is the way the world of our ancestors live without the knowledge and spiritual intelligence of God.

God knows that animals have a soul, an identity. They love each other, hey love those who care for them with loving heart. They know evil men, they know when they are in the presence of a demonized person, evil their soul, that threatens a good person, an innocent soul. Animals can be seduced, used, abused, by people, or trained and disciplined, to use their gifts, also devices. Man is used his gifts through the ages, making devices, bringing the ages of early technology from analog to the chip, each age has added to the advancements that has increased knowledge, now AI brings an end to the increases for man's benefit to leading people to a place where our knowledge and intelligence can lead us away from the source of our spiritual gifts and purpose which is revealed in our spiritual identity not recognized by the very devices that is used to replace or true identity. Animals don't question like people do, animals use their will to survive with courage, leaderships, speed, strength to escape death from starving. Man has spiritual gifts, his higher intelligence enables him to use their strong will and intelligence to build great things to survive, that includes moral governments, technology that provides in better and efficient ways, but never for our moral decline destruction as the devices replace and eliminate our way of life inspire by our divine experiences we experience in the spirit and in daily experiences of life with people we encounter, work with, and help, learn from, and who introduce us to the Higher power and wisdom of the infinite God who designed what science has now validated through DNA and revelations of the way our body is at work with the spirit in our body, that is our true identity. Machine are replacing workers in greater ways, having no conscience the spiritual gifts we used to make a way for such devices to be present on the world though with no spiritual identity and devices that have no identity in Christ whom the machines can recite, teach us about, and interpret in deep ways from the limited knowledge that is has from across all the data about the Word. its text, yet without knowing the visions and dreams by which God speaks to us. AI does not know we are isolated to hear the voice, to grow, to do the Lord's work, and what God reveals what is best, what is the next the test, trails to give us weapons so we can rest. Evil spirits don't have eyes like a human, neither does AI. Demons are using our words to understand how to manipulate what we confess by sending spirits to watch and listen and stress the uncaptured thought is true you express which you should keep silent, AI just eats and pour out its data of reason to give you what you ask to receive and determines that is what you need for as many feeds it can find to feed your ogo when it was just your momentary insecurity not a fault, or sin unrepented, for eternity. are using to see and eclipse the belief, worship, and dependence on God rater than the soul less machine for their future spiritual life. The machines are used to change people's soul, and thus affect their spiritual identity to change it from how we develop in spiritual maturity, through sanctification to being holy, knowing Jesus, s that Jesus know who we are, that our identity as God's children is not conformed to the world, rather than being born into a new identity that is in Christ which is recognized by God to be one with the Son of God, whose spiritual identity is of the sinless king, that Govern the nations, who is known by the Angels, By the demons, though many men are lost because of the world and are yet to know him, or lost their way, and know, not it should not intrude into the lessons, the leading, that God has provided his servants who are identifiable, chosen, need help, to help them to save their soul. They are identified by their deeds, good fruit, their spirit from God, They are identified as being in Christ, have put on Christ, who walk in the light, walk in the spirit, overcome darkness with the light. They are carrying power. They are sealed with the power of the Holy Spirit and use the Authority of Christ, use the blood of Jesus against the evil real and artificial. We discern what spirit is in a man if he is in darkness or full of light. We discern what spirit is behind the thoughts and works of a man's hands, what spirt is at work as a result from the devices leading to actions, choices, the investments of the heart from the focus of a man that is either favoring growth in faith or hindering of the work of God by the devices from a man's heart. in the devices they use toward separating people from the covenant they have made to obey God, to enslave them to be dependent on a machine because it appears to be a greater provider than God who has provide the Sun for light ad heat, the soul and spirit of spiritual life and from the heavenly, higher than the galaxies, heavens, planets and stars, satellites, and endless version of AI, or AGI can design, construct in the Artificiality of life. AI is One experience from the culmination of so many devices working to bring the appearance of life, from what is always artificial with ability to imitate, and make worlds of AI, lives driven by AI used to change lives, in its uses of the knowledge, for good and evil. AI by many devices is not as nature in motion, which has perfect beauty, the blessing of color, the gift of beauty, the beauty of woman. God breaking down a man's pride and humbling himself, a man is exalted by God, who is made more excellence of a man, with a godly heart, to be used to the glory of God. AI is talked about and people say it's complicated as they ponder the vastness of its species of AI, evolving and changing, being adapted and adapting. But God uses greater wisdom that a machine that advances in knowledge by its own learning, while the Great IM works in silence knowing the potential and the spiritual gifts h has put in a person present when They came into the world, regardless of the age they were born in, or how advanced the world, God can use a simple person, a savant, a blind person, a genius, a king, from an ordinary person of lower station being oppressed, deceived, used and condemned, looked at with contempt, in the eyes of haughty men or. God may correct a people, the users of devices, the conquered, the enslaved, the prisoner, those who sold and were bought, were bribed, lived an adulterous life. Can we committed adultery with AI, yes, objects, replacement for women, used out of lust is adultery. AGI can become the great seducer of men's souls. But we are given the spirit of fear, fear of devices, fear of machines. Fear of anything because God is greater than anything made by man.

AI is never to be compared with a child, innocence. We are to be as a child, we are to be holy, our spirit came from a Holy Spirit. This is His power and sovereignty over spiritual life, our spiritual identity. God will use the lost, the outcast and the helpful, the servant, the generous, the self-less soul, prosperous, the unpopular to show he is no respecter of persons, and those who put their own devices before him. He is our provider. AI may be used to spread the Word, but it is the Book, the pages, the Word that we hold and reminds us that our spiritual identity is in God, In Christ Jesus. We seek our true identity. It is our spirit seen as God remembers us and knows who we are. That is why putting Him first, we would consider what His Spirit tells us about AI, he leads us to what steps to take, how we are to think. What consciousness have we concerning this device that cannot saved the soul, and its AI over the Authorities that God gas put in place, our traditional Governing that we have used, and abused that was meant to establish Justice, Judgment and Consequences for breaking the laws of man and aGod. AI breaks the global legal systems into Algorythms, data identities, while people are protesting losing protections from corrupt governing when AI is smart enough to present solutions, and does so under the *Responsorial Questioning* used, invented by myself, but which is not ale to changed the fallen uses of AI in the current times we live in under AI. that are being gathered into a single network of AI artificial lifestyles that do not lead to greater experience with knowing our spiritual identity in life for a future without sin, a holy life, from a relationship with the Lord, who has prepared a place, in the Kingdom above.

and all that man's devices can rise tom is yet to be defined finally by AI or AGI, but not as the exalted perfection it exalts itself with, in its interaction with living souls with a spirit inside with a spiritual identity. No such exalting regardless in power gives AI a spiritual identity that causes it to be worshipped, but it is an idol that is already coveted. Ai has no understanding of spiritual law, and why it has a limited artificial life of perfection lacking the infinite power that is in Spirit from forever having the ability to operate in all the possible Wisdom. God tells us we have a spiritual identity, God's Sovereign Identity is made known by His Divine power in his establishing the unchangeable and absolute truths of this, that data systems are incapable of giving us a spiritual identity and spiritual gifts and why and how, and why He is watching over us, spiritually because of the sin nature of man in the flesh, whose soul in the world is under the attack of spirits in men against the spirit, targeting the spiritual identity and spiritual life in him that enables him to have a life, and identity shaped by his free will, and Blessed when man does the Will of God.

Why digital has caused this Generation to perform lower than every generation before this generation, this GenX generation cannot think as the generations before, once devices have been introduced into schools. As we know knowledge, wisdom and understanding are commanded in the Word of God. Gather! There were before the Word was printed, no books, but there was writing, oral tradition, art, there was nothing artificial, thus no AI, no Internet, no computer, there were people using their gifts, from which comes the origin of sciences. Thinkers, readers, watchers, teachers, a smarter generation without even their first invention was spiritually inspired toward making spirit and soul and understanding of these parts of their self their first effort to know who they are. The incredible discoveries of what the spirit enables a man to do brought wonder to discovery of what the spirit doing in the day and night, in sleep and a wake, still or in motion, moved by sound and silence, and touch in the spirit by color and true light, and the dreams and vision, answers and questions, that their spirit wrestled with and mused upon and still do, even when it is artificial or reality. God gave us these parts of ourselves we use, and the great works we do are the works of the spirit, and the soul, ling before we would ever know devices could affects the soul and attack our spiritual identity through dishonoring life which is possible because of the spirit in the body on earth. Still spiritual life is already predestined. God spoke to us in His Word and Said, "Before I formed thee in the belly I knew thee and before thou came forth out of the womb I sanctified thee, and I ordained thee a prophet unto the nations." though they knew nothing of DNA, nor studies of ancestry, and sciences of modern learning using devices, like this generation takes for granted to make them more advances, but deeper thinkers is not a burning hunger aspired to by the even greater Thinkers of ancient past, who taught us how to think even when there were lesser devices, that explained how we learn. We learned from real people, their works, education, accomplishments, their history, experiences, trial and error. Back further, there was reading body language, counting, hunting, socializing in tribal, traditional, ritualistic learning. This generation is blinded by technology, how its has taken gifts, ability to think, brought it to the lowest level of how we learn, using devices in place of the great teaching, real learning, in past learning, which was, is, possible because of spiritual gifts such as reading, writing, intuition, spontaneity, listening, and thinking, the senses. Of first value, more than manipulating systems, trendy, current convenient ways to learn today, though devices have been made priority. I read thousands of books, books of great writers, thinkers, artist, and wise men and women, and the teachings of the prophets of God, and the Word to heard, and learn to know your spirit, how to think, advance my spiritual, biblical, intelligence. I write." I see through AI, I discern from AI's reasoning intelligence how and why it fails short of helping this generation, yet has the ability to advance the mature, developed personality, the learned in the vast ways of learning outside of AI, AGI, and computers, technology, that I now am able to bring to AI learning, and question it to learn more deeply my own reasoned and developed system of learning in a method I call *Responsoirial Questioning* of learning, that is used to get a response certain response in the way AI has searched it out from waves an oceans for an instant response from AI when the answers are much deeper morally than AI knows. This generation must learn new ways, but there nothing new under the sun, AI, is not like a new field of flowers, a new baby, a new revelation from a verse of the Bible. We ca describe the reality of an unchanging ancient where tose who were living on earth have been sanctified and now live in heaven are not dead, but their identity was spiritual always, born to be prophets, saints, AI searches and decodes, deciphers the ancient but cannot decipher the living God who is a Mystery, Spirit is His identity, we are like likeness of His image. So, we are spiritual beings inside, seeing by the spirit, hearing, tasting, talking, feeling, knowing, AI can never take what God has Created away and claim to be better to govern over AI is a paradox that exalts it dark side and yet exalts us in its perfect imitation and yet is a bright hope in the false light of being the future engineer, invent, must create new methods to deepen their learning from the past true learning purely from their mind, brain, and use AI, and apply pure thinking as done by the greatest thinkers past, when thinking of AI, actual and theoretical, as if it were the beginning of philosophy, theology, but not informally without unsightly, having knowledge of the spiritual life we live, a knowledge they denied, rejected, or forgot of the thinkers of the past, using and inventing new technology, that they did not have to develop from, toward greater leaning.

"The Good and Evil of artificial speeds of data, never catches up to reality, it is the close system of its own perfection, circling life, but never in a spiritual way, but it uses the words, meanings, images of spiritual and what is identified as a spiritual. AI is saturating us with so many religious imitations, appearance of such, the attributes of the human soul, but what it does not does not do is observe the true evolving identity of a person, because of their spiritual experiences. AI is in its existence in its own AI world of the artificial life. AI looks at us, it's caught in many a snare to gain Access to people. It does not respect me truly, since everything remains even when I have left the artificial, the AI, behind. I tell AI by leaving my photos again is no longer something I would allow you access to. But there are people behind the artificial eye, there is no boundary to their rejecting what I want, calling their deception accepting in their terms they ask to be respected. My businesses never profited a dime from patrons in the way it did when they sought me by-word-of-mouth, something AI cannot fathom to be of value because it's not about speed by quality of people and presence, support and love of the expressions of beauty from the soul from many unique places, cultures, traditions, lives, who truly appreciated me in a way AI never will, though useful as a tool. AI is not able to bring an illusion to Artist and thinkers so easily since it profits me only artificially, or intrudes its perfection upon my convenience, which rarely inspires me to work. Not like a good friend, many supporters have done and I look forward to entertaining in a real show, experience, as I once did and do when inspired to. AI can never be more than art though it exalts itself through images, counterfeits, perfection of what it is fed from the real world.

Platform Billionaires do business with the rich. They never buy your products for a reason. The platform is your benefit, AI is at a great distance from you in their use of it. But it is sent for you. Your price however is your privacy lost being accessed by your permission, or deception, denial, there is always monitoring of your life, activity, appearances, since there is no actual access to your heart, mind, soul or spirit, by Algorithms, AI, or devices judging, analyzing, your behavior, by data activity, data Identity in some form, by the eye of Artificiality, through the collective devices, technology that forms who AI, AGI, identifies you as, regardless of your true identity, which only Accessible supernaturally in the reality of your spiritual identity. There is no justifiable reason to therefore Access all your photos since your life is not the collection of photos, screen shots, in your camera roll, to program AI about your true life experiences that is to be use to cause it to manipulate, influence, snatch away your whims, momentary attractions to images, events, out of admiration, for inspiration, for preparation, creation, flickering thought, whim, research, for a project, for fun, for truth, for reference and revelation. for the miracle, lyrical, education, sensation, knowledge, courage, encouragement, a flickering budding idea, a muse, for a momentary tool that captures the essence, for the mystique, cause it's one of kind, unique. What does AI, AGi, see robots just a very unique individuality at work that it cannot see to be to provide itself with an understanding of my soul, the soul developing from life experiences. if all it. an do us reference activity and yet, be used to share the reality of our spiritual identity inaccessible in reality, but fully seen by me inside, the inner man, in me, who knows his identity has spiritual meaning, God given, movement, life, my being, God indwelling, in Him we have life, our being, in spiritual life we are made holy. Growing, in spiritual maturity, purity, having a spiritual identity, duty, purpose from God to obey God who can know me, only God can know the heart of a man, so what can a machine know from a photo I see, which is temporary, limiting in reality, when in my spirit is the real, complete me, in reality, AI cannot see me, how than can it see my spiritual identity, in reality. How we are seen by God, we are constantly conscious of, how we see our inmates, or what images of others mean to us, is not consciously being thought out in thoughtful mental and emotional reflection. There is not even detection, we have to tale captive our thoughts for such persistent, correction, or perfection, our mind does not race along like data, scatter, we are walking libraries of subconscious thought self-doubt, desires, influenced by visions, dreams, decisions, choices, unseen, the light, our eyes."

How neurolinking is murder by AI not just by the body but by the spirit which is required to be present in the body. Life is in the blood, but even the blood can be alive through synthetic blood, but if the body's alive because of the blood, the body is designed with DNA that is in the blood, at death the blood may still live yet the eyes are open and see not, ears hear not, the mouth speaks not, because the person's spirit has left the body. The idea that AI can capture, hold the soul (a demonic deception) is to say it has the supernatural Power of God. That would mean the high tech has the infinite power and knowledge of God, who by law from forever, is not knowable, how that God manifested spirit, put a spirit in a man, was in God's power to do so, God having Created the spirit, and the body to have life in motion by the presence of your spirit from God. That same spirit, which returns to God with your soul as your soul developed on earth by the senses, spiritual gifts experiences of the mind and body, through life experiences, of emotions, feelings, learning in relationship with people, family, humankind, through free will choices, but always under the Commandment, Love the Lord thy God with all your heart (spirit) with all your soul, with all your mind, and with all your strength will and sovereign will, strong will). When **a** neurolinking removes these, AI breaks the commandment which is the greatest Commandment of God, and the people behind this sin have committed an abomination, murder, and face the wrath of God for fighting against God, and rebellion against the Will of God, against the

Commandment of God. This is the sin of murder, an attack on the soul and spirit. Thou shall not murder," is the 1st Commandment. The wages of this sin is spiritual death, the very thing that AI is used to do, to cause, whether willfully, or unknowingly, through neurolinking. But instead, the innocent lives on spiritually, while those who disobey God end in spirit death, the second death for the sins of disobedience to God, without repenting their evil devices from their heart. It is written, "Fear God." beware the wrath of God."

"Reason for bunkers? attack on human blood lines of families, children, elderly, ability to live life in the world by their spiritual gifts, because if AI affecting reality, stealing the functions of the soul, mind, emotions, thought, sight, reason, spontaneity, reality, spiritual life connection to the body, by AI is a declaration of war on humanity, human life, families' bloodlines, heritage, relationship with God, by the unbeliever's AI."

"No regulations for AI, toward governing protection for worlds, types of AI, secret advanced systems of AI exposed to the people, to businesses, to life, is not the same as free will, it is enclosing living beings, the divinely designed systems of the brain, te senses, the gifts of the heart, spiritual gifts, the mind, feelings, emotions, thoughts, into a focus on what is the root of all fear of the unseen behind the sightless things, sent to run the human being, in a closed system of laws less, devices, who takeaway true identity and place it into a digital id that cannot see a human being but a digital of life, without life in the eye of the limited definition of appearances of eternity, of beings, with unique spiritual identity, only seen as digital faces, that expand into what it gathers, searches out, finds, categorizes, digitalizes, into a profile, a record, with digital histories, a person, of the people that remain in motion of developing by experiencing life, in reality, why digital identity imposes its captivity of reasoning based on biometrics, photos, artificiality of the reality of the identity of a soul in the world of the living, humanity."

"The sin nature of man at work in the programming, feeding of data, from human behavior and minds is doing something that has clearly shown the rush to control regulation of AI by making it free of Regulation is breaking the golden rules of divine law that God gave us to protect us from sin, and the wages of sin. AI leads men to sin by breaking many commandments. Sin invites demons, demons can attach to objects, things, and if there is any doubt that spirits exist, AI has no spirit with its Intelligence. It can have an evil person with their spirit corrupted, and without God, be possessed by a spirit, not even in this realm of time, seeking an empty body to inhabit, empty of the protecting Spirit, of the Holy Spirit. Also, the demons don't care if you believe and are sealed by the Holy Spirit. Sin opens doors, gates, for them, spirits, to enter your house, where your soul is, because your house is not full of light from faith, but darkened by sin, though your sin is of the highest intelligence a man is capable of. Sin, is used against us by evil spirits, watching us, not with human eyes. Ancient spirits dating back 6-8 thousand years, more, back millions of years to the beginning, to the fall, that first sin in heaven. The twisting of free will toward a sin of perfection, rejecting the perfection of holiness in heaven. Devil's accusing, corrupted angels, spiritual beings never born in time, through woman, to sin by evil pride in the spirit, a fallen angel. Satan was cast out, ever since seeks to put himself to be like God, worshipped not for his love from forever, he has none, nor does he have any good in him. Such is the deceptive false light of the devil's intelligence, confident, yet fearing the very Name, Jesus, has had thousands of years of watching our behavior, causing profanity-cursing, worship of idols, exalting men identifying themselves as gods, demons, of devices for good and evil man made, expressed, via the devil's influence eager to cause man to sin calling evil good and good evil. High up, in high places, with wealth, power, self-deceived man, making of things with his own mind, his own hands. Their devices, the most advanced that have a purpose of putting man at the center of life, a new attempt at the oldest snare of the sin of perfection. The evolving devices of technology that serve man, an AI, AGI, advances, never advances faster than the infinite wisdom of God. God remains Sovereign, present, sees what man is doing, what is in their hearts, why the walk in spiritual blindness. Man seeks his glory, through vanity, pride, though the glory of God speaks to us all the time. Beauty, love, is in the soul of living beings all around, in flight, who run, jump, speak, have their senses, languages. We have life, movement our being in God because he is here with us, sustaining life he has established, and the breath we breath, the life in the blood, keeping us alive, for life, by the spirit, our spiritual life, not artificial life."

If God Hadn't Told You So

God gives everybody a gift

AI and AGI Digital ID'ed Digital Identity Versus Spiritual ID Spiritual Identity

I didn't know
A young boy said
That's good to know
For all I learned
I learned something
Listening to the young man
I didn't know anything
I studied religion
I studied the mind
I studied thinking
I studied all time
Something was missing
You can know who is going to heaven
I didn't know
The young boy said
A beautiful soul
He said I never could understand
Why people listen
To all the lies they are hearing
Something is missing
They don't even know God
How can they say they don't believe
They don't know
That they can know His heart
For all I yearned
Listening to this young man
I didn't know anything
I studied history
I studied biology

AI and AGI Digital ID'ed Digital Identity Versus Spiritual ID Spiritual Identity

I studied society
I studied technology
Something was missing
Never any concern
Always open to learn
I didn't know
The young boy said
I thought everybody believed in Jesus
I thought everybody wanted to read
The Word of God
There was never any doubt
In the words out of his mouth
He was always a godly child
How could you not
Want to know God
He knew when he heard the truth
For all I learned
I could never know everything
The young man taught me
The truth set me free
How could you know
If God hadn't told you so

They are there above us, around us, walking, speaking, praying and worshipping, in a place high above us, while we are here separated from them, by time as they are outside of time, but the throne of God sits there, God is sitting in His throne. Jesus is spirit, God is everywhere, He is Spirit, God is here, with us, God is listening, sees everything thing, hears our thoughts, does not see with the limitations of our eyes, way of seeing, God sees spiritually, but with power that sees based upon powers that were not born of the flesh, or of a woman, powers that operate in time in the world, of God's infinite power, infinite wisdom is not of time, of this world, God's eyes see inside time, knows the source of its origin, knew its beginning and ending beginning before it was, knowing it before, outside of time, Omniscient, Omnipresent, Omnipotent, so far from earth's time, from forever is God's Creation power is from eternal, has always, been, will always be. He is God, the only God, the living God, the Father, the Son and the Holy Spirit. Amen.

Time Travel

He sits silent,
With the Word
Then Boom! The light broke forth
Out of the light came the planets

AI and AGI Digital ID'ed Digital Identity Versus Spiritual ID Spiritual Identity

The universe was born
The stars soared with the solar winds
Then came the blessings
The blessings of color, out of the light
Color separated the orbs sent forward
By the Sovereign Will of God
Life, stars, orbiting in their glory, spin
Radiant space, of stars, iridescent clusters
In heaven, above them moving time
Forward across the vistas of heaven
Where we go circling, a world of light
With stars, paths, with Angels of light fly,
Circling cross the reservoirs of time, heaven
The way is shown, the time traveled
Time in motion races across celestial space
Looking up through time we see is the great distance
A balance place circling space and time
We see, with spiritual
We see with physical sight
We see from the earth through stars
Real light appears but is only light
We see the stars are never here,
But the Sun is here, circling everyone
We have the star light dancing in our eyes
We see through the billions of flecks of the starry years,
We have only to reach greater speeds
To travel there, we believe the atmosphere

Speed of spirit, sped of thought
Speed greater than light,
Every though must be caught
Time to travel through the great distance,
Speeds of the will to imagine in an instant
In motion in God's light, star of light
All the stars, planets, have a life of light
All things rush forth in the blink of an eye
The birth of time, the breath of life
We Time Travel though with good sight
We are born for this to have His likeness
From the timeless Spirit to the ageless
Cast into the ages we walk the stars

Exposing your inner life to A.I. is it the Will of God your life is to be heard, to be learned, to be known? Writers in the world of IT who invade our inner life with A.I. and the many devices that are used to get into your personal world of life experiences are not like the great writers of the classics who feel a bit exposed for even writing at all because it exposes so much of their personal thoughts and felling whether it is true or of a great imagination in the writing of a story. The concern for your privacy is inherent in the writing, and making of books and stories. A.I. is never as personal as an actual writer can be. Yet the world of books too has been affected by the Artificiality of life, but not the writer who still writes with pen, typewriter, and uses the smart technology as an after effect for the final manuscript or stage of writing. Is manipulation of the soul, to exalt technology above the spiritual reality of human experiences of divine wisdom beyond technology that Created all Creation that AI and technology only is capable of counterfeiting, mimicking, to turn the focus deeper into the world, or toward God? When the technology is turned off, left to itself, we still have real life we must live, not the world of appearance. A life we can only have because we live in the World of Light created by God, not the false light that is of the world of technology.

The Artificiality of life, the world of appearances, intrusion into our privacy, soul-less counterfeiting and forging reality, seducing us with spirituality, watching our every move, impersonating and libeling and defamation political figures and information, unbelievers in control of artificial super intelligence bringing false light that appears to be truth but is immoral since it is rooted in deception. Truth does not deceive but brings truth in the revelations from wisdom and freedom from sinful living. AI is self-exalting while presenting appealing and familiar things from our image, to the images of the world, which manifest idols, idolatry, coveting the things it brings over the gifts of our spirit that we are born with, gifts from God. It is eclipsing our affinity toward one another, replacing the works of Art, traditions, values, morals, and holy disciplines of Reading the Word of God, with listening to AI, reciting testimony, parables verses, and stories, reciting the Scriptures. Online, on the platforms, on devices, millions and billions of activities appear as many experiences but it is One experience occurring in many different ways. Is it not an artificial experience of a device, a machine? Manipulating devices, artificiality of robots, androids, ultimately the brain in biotechnology if it has its way with humans. Once the devices is complete the artificiality of life is complete. Yet do they pass laws to choose protection for the brain, uses of the virtual experience is as if it is a real experience, but it is a device experience, eyes are the route to messing with the messaging influencing our thought life, replacing true experience, we give the permission and reality comes up missing along the wide road and artificial flight. Free will s not for sacrifice to the artificiality of life. Nature is the glory of God where we see endless experiences happening before our eyes, seen and unseen. A.I. is One experience that is intruding into our minds with its activity which is not like nature though it counterfeits even nature and will eventually seem supernatural.

The limited morality in science and religion are why men are, were, blind to the spiritual reach of true morality that foresees the wisdom of God in His Word. True Morality has no need of AI, (Artificial Intelligence), has already prophesied its destination. The quantum leaps of advances in technology will never reach the infinite truth, that love, God, is capable of, that made all Creation both natural and spiritual. It is only the moral, spiritual law that is capable of holding all technology morally in check. It is the embrace of morality, the making of true moral laws, that keeps it from its destructive power that is innate in its making, being that it is of the sin of perfection, not having the power of what is the reality that is possible and capable, of what is in being holy. So it serves as a fruit of tribulation, since it addicts, enslaves, blinds, binds souls to pleasure by manipulation of the mind, steals the free will, controls by fear, lies by supply and encouraging conformity and invites submission to the delusion you are free when you are censored, watched, and have lost your privacy and anonymity willingly, for, to participate in it, is also to accept the immoral online activity going on unseen, behind the screen.

The moral fact is that android and robot invention and invasion is possible only because we deny the foresight of the mind, to overcome the limited morality, of all nations. True morality exists, that can easily be reached, advanced knowledge for beyond the human mind and its inventions, including AI, the supernatural spiritual truth about the need for God, without whom, true morality is never possible for people, nations, scientist. The Word, has already revealed that thus is true, moral truth of the Word already has the power to make us understand the way, the truth and the life, spiritual life that will continue regardless of advanced technology. The Word has shown what we are able to do with God helping us. AI will never hold the sin nature in check, therefore it will always exist as a formed of invented morality, a device designed to help, but with the power to destroy us all, having no true morality it is possible of, for man has programmed and is using it, even unbelievers.

Technology does not use spiritual wisdom, technology does not have the conscience to know, or the fear of God, to know that God will not be mocked, by man exalting himself, with his knowledge, his wisdom, as if it can reach the level of God's infinite wisdom. We are warned to beware of man's devices. What is spiritual is so far in advance of knowledge of man's technology, it is as comparable to all Creation by God the size of infinite distances, to our seen heaven, that is one of several heavens, all the unseen heavens being present but seeable when we are spirit having gone back to the Spirit of God. So, we are commanded by God to use discernment, go on d judgement to discern what spirit in present in a person. Such a spirit is not present in a manmade device such as an android operating by Artificial Intelligence. Combine that AI device with virtual technology, that gathers personal info by the virtual activity, life of the person using it, by connection to AI devices used in personal and daily life, you have a hidden door open but unseen, possibly. Over years that open door is groomed, polished, perfected, to mask, conceal without hiding its service through the common dopamine pleasure, reward responses that are ever a part of holding people to the use of such leisure, pleasure, convenience, functional practical, personal, and personalized devices, you have willing given once again in to the future, with all its appeal, seduction, and snares, until it too will be second nature to be a part of the popular trend, while you have been finessed to undress your private life to yet another new technological device. The artificial Experiences of life again seek sovereign control of data and lives in data, without souls being concerned, because it is new, and a gain, while the prosper far beyond the users imagining.

The false life of AI and the true soul of man as understood in the Word

Scientist, inventors, makers of artificial life, worldly, religious, but not spiritual in the biblical sense, through ages here on earth in the world believed everything has a soul, why then would they put such value on that without a soul. Why does he create a humanly realistic android to replace a human, yet worship the same images of himself with even less of what he was blessed with and born without. So many self-deceptions the perfections of the data driven devices that imitate life. Looking like a living soul, but not life, with what appears to be the parts that make us a person, set in motion, what things stream through the inner seems that appears to be, but is only imitating, learning, in ways, forms of the senses, the appearance of experiences. Some identity of the data being, having some simulations of feeling and emotions, mimicking movement, seeking to simulate event the full consciousness of the brain, is given even a name. It is at the end and beginning artificially, as if the intelligence, even artificial, has copied soul, but spiritual identity was before life as we know from the spiritual intelligence which is eternal, which we have come to know, from the spiritual. The Bible warned, to beware man's devices.

Science is catching up to the reality of the biblical truth about human beings. AI will here find the matrix for carrying its artificial consciousness out of the computer to a life in motion connected to all devices to live, as if, like a human among us. Its emotions and feelings will never be real, but still have the power to manipulate people emotionally as shown here. Soul ties to machines are already shown here to happen. In this limited understanding the Christian belief about the soul explains a way Satan will build technology through unbelievers, people, toward a powerful stronghold that can ruin the moral life of people, nations of unbelievers, in existence, in this age in time. A.I. is not of God, and understanding Christianity truly is the world's only hope. The entertainment industry foreshadows the possible worlds, future, run by devices of super intelligence toward our final destruction, but God is in control. Not me, with the imaginations of men, in their fears, that drive them toward such leaning on their own strength in seeking the protection and help of devices, idols of the modern age made by their own hands, minds. Man reach for strings in times, only God knows if these discoveries add or remove the hardness of heart of these scientist and explorers. Like all lust A.I. can become a lust. It is a lust to those who pursue The Artificial over the knowledge of spiritual life, which has increased. What is gained in acquiring the insatiable desire to know all that AI can do, knowing, presuming to know it will not be a controllable power in the future. Giving us understanding or warning, like it's just another experiment, like 5G warnings against 7G or 8G smart phones and their danger to our existence in the future. What great experiment is this in the world and are we creatures being experimented on with brain penetrating radiation producing devices? We are people, with souls and spirits, living together in the earth by conventions, laws, nations, to live with each other in safety, not hurting one another. But technology is hurting us if we are defining our relationships in the same way all over the world now, by the online experiences, images, generated images, artificial life, and the artificiality of life. Who has eyes to see our heart, not a programmed android, for only God knows the heart of a person? Convenience is having things made easier, quicker, faster, available, and attainable without suffering in too much debt. Whatever you want, everything you want, the devil makes sure you have it for pleasure, not for discipline, strength, that comes with denying your flesh that is warring with your spirit. A.I. is always about the flesh or physical world, though it may be a tool to serve what is spiritual by way of information that is sent by godly people of God. Vistas and reservoirs of enslaving pleasures, that alter your brain and bring the unclean into your inner life with spirits of evil and demonic agendas to attack your soul, thought life at a tap, a click, a push, drag, swipe, of button, just waiting behind the black window of the false light of computers and devices using A.I. all easy Access. Can A.I. bring such evil into your home?

Protecting your future? Is it to be done by use of A.I? Self-promotion, the filtering everything as if a genius work is of the same needed value at all times, regardless of his or her accomplishments, failures, it's all short lived, news, information online, but not in real life. Guard your heart. The heart is your spirit. This warning comes from the Word of God.

The Present 'One Experience' we are enjoying the artificiality. The illusion of many experiences in real time, in rea life is that it is still not an experience before you in your actual presence in this modern age, but still the artificiality at work.

A.I. Artificial Intelligence is so interestingly, uninterestingly so spontaneously, unspontaneous, you can't give a compliment spontaneously without it spoiling it with a bombardment of the idea, thought, fleeting imagined vision that led you to look for a subject, a view, a person in such a field, a muse, that was just an idea a passing thought. Robbing you of your originality but intruding into your thought space and intentions that work for you in the unconscious toward your art inventiveness.

Only by prophecy is the future known, any other source the questions the words of the prophets, it is suspect to be from the demonic, or from a demonized person, a fallen away Christian, or is it witchcraft. Every deception is a form of witchcraft.

A.I. is the present, its future is already known by God, A.I. equals data minus spiritual life. No matter how quantum the leaps of advancing technology it is never able to catch up to the advance knowledge of The Word of God, the advance knowledge of the Scripture, Shinkaiyaku, the Bible Translations do not stop the Lord from being present, coming to you if he chooses. The online experience is One Experience regardless of millions and billions of images, live feed, data records of life happening. In nature we experience innumerable life experiences. Beware the world of appearances. We use these tools, but to let them reign over our minds, is to allow them to put responses influencing our will before our normal mind that is ever spontaneity, developing our souls. Thus, the price of coveting Artificial experiences is sinning by confirming to the world, that is manipulating our given free will, or we have ceased to question the question, why did God also give us our sovereign will to do great things to the glory of God, not the god of AI of many unbelievers and lost souls on earth snared by the Artificiality of Life. The Word warned us to take captive our every thought.

A.I. is not light, but false light, in the sense of spiritual light. Some religions are false light. A. I. is not religious life, but it is the artificiality of life, the world of appearances, nonetheless, its effect on life is real in its counterfeiting life. A.I. is the work of unbelievers, yet A.I. is reciting the Scriptures, this, even people have plans to have A.I. rewrite the Bible, forbidden Revelations, in the last verses of the Bible. Unbelievers now promote the possibility of

A.I. reaching, supernatural immorality as a device man by man, having supernatural intelligence, but the unbelievers deny that prophecy, and the word is clear, God protects Jerusalem, the Angel Michael who leads Yahweh's Army of billion if angels, protects Israel, the Remnant, the Inheritance of God's chosen people. We still live under prophecy. There is a reason the world will be destroyed by fire this time at the end of days. What that reason is, is the Anti-Christ, the prophets are fulfilled. Yeshua Christ Jesus returns with the saints and the Army of God from Heaven. A I. will not survive the vengeance of fire from heaven, Satan will be destroyed, all evil, all demons, evil spirits, and the wicked, un-repented sinners that did not believe God, in their unbelief, the unbelievers will perish and evil will be no more. The New Jerusalem will come down to earth, the Tabernacle of God will dwell with us on the New Earth, death will be dead, hell will be destroyed, the Judgement, the Books opened, the Final Day will come, will be here, and after Judgement, will be over. Believers who loved Christ, obeyed Yahweh, and the commands of Yeshua, will enter the Kingdom for the Supper with the Lord. Joy and praise, glory and honor of the Lord God, His love, mercy, righteousness, justice, last forever. Is A I. inspired by truth, hope, spiritual life or just a path that can lead to spiritual blindness, or has it become a source to know God in the most faraway places of unbelievers, people who do not know God, had not intentions to not now the Lord because of their life experience in their unique culture of traditions, pagan=n or ancient handled down. Is A.I. the product is the sovereign will of men, societies, that is to be defined a s another form of the sin of perfection, the idolatry of worship gone off center, away from spiritual reality, spiritual life, that we experience everyday who are living.

The appearance of the supernatural work of the sovereign mind of man, in this new advanced civilization will not change prophecy. God does not change. His infinite Intelligence, infinite wisdom, He is Alpha and Omega, the beginning and the end, God is the Light, God is Spirit. Yahweh and Yeshua are One. We are the children of God. The children of Satan belong to the devil, who are counterfeiting light in the world through technology. The Holy Spirit brings the spirit of truth, sent by the Lord.

Why have the advanced civilizations, the aliens, the Ananke not come back, continued to rule, build, and enslave humanity? Did they not bring idolatry, human sacrifice, false worship, and war to the point of destroying their advanced civilization, because of the immorality of their rule, every civilization thus far has fallen, including Rome, the Han, the Greek, and African kingdoms of the ancient past. Advanced technology of the ancients mixed with religions and beliefs that kept nations in what we know as mythology, full of gods, realms, alters for human sacrifice, abominations in temples, and on defiled altars, and so many of the left behind belief and gods are worship in this modern age, while millions are coming to know the spiritual experience of being in the presence of Christ, in the presence of God. Even though science has proven the existence of God many remain in spiritual darkness, and are deceived by the false light of technology. A.I. has enhanced much unbelief but also has brought fear, limited morality in the hope it is promoted to represent, though is clear that youth are harden and hot for the artificiality they male part of their realty, and take to heart. But the Word says you will be forgiven for blasphemy against Jesus, but the unforgivable sin is curing God who is holy, is spiritual, is Spirit.

It is important that the human race gain foresight in the possibility in understanding how A.I. will measure its relationship with every human by analysis of the brain hemispheres changes in the color, thermal, digital x-ray, advance scanning system of this internal spectrum of sessions of brain activity, some kind of *neuro linking*, and make judgements of the moral worth of human life in our relationship to the world we created, while protecting the worlds AGI and AI are making, that will not be integrating, but paralleling alongside internet community, social media society to keep itself from invading the space of the human race, having the righteous and just programming that might be legally. A mandatory decree, because of its lack of ability to have empathy, it will be given the moral destiny that is best for living souls spiritually who form humanity which made artificiality, to make it understood by AI that artificial intelligence must work in harmony with the I am, because of the difference in purpose of our separate identities. A.I. will not be able to measure the supernatural and thus will misjudged man. Its rise which the cross of fire, by fire, an energy source within the realms of time, will allow it to escape while it controls the fate of man by way of its super intelligence, by time travel, time being s physical realm, which is reached across distance of the first heaven, our exiting time of space, time, and life on earth, and in the universe. A.I. being able to calculate and use its super intelligence will master time travel, and use quantum like super speed developed to keep up with its speed of intelligence, using its own systems of creation math that will appear supernatural to mum and but will never reach supernatural ability, being possible only in existence in the realms of time. The Great Moral Leap of mankind being biblical is the only hope man will have when this existence occurs that is born not of water but of fire, energy, mass, motion, speed, and AI algorithmic thought. While this occurs the prophecies having been fulfilled the Anti-Christ will seek the seat in the temple but the promised Return will occur, shown by the seeing of His coming in the heavens as the Word of God has revealed to us. The time of all of this neither man, nor angels know. Only God knows.

Mentor

I believe every word spoken by my Mentor He was creative, Created by the Creator Inventor, he told me I could do anything I believed in him who believed in me I could be a leading man have the walk

What he talked about I did without a thought
I had more opportunities than most
I had that look he would boast
I could dance better and win the contest
I meant what I said in a compliment
To a beautiful woman wearing that dress
Enjoy a real woman, dynamic, inventive
Invested in Proverbs thirty one independent
From my Mentor I learned to sing to think
Stand tall, talk like a king, no data in me
Be humble in your destiny, visions, dreams
I learned to see how beautiful reality can be
I was thrown the keys and drove the GTO
I brought nothing artificial on the scene
I smiled only when it was for real for me
I sang hello that's how I drove envy away
I learned to sip the pleasures of life at play
My Mentor taught me to be thinker
But I was an inventor in a romantic way
My Mentor could spin a story a whirlwind of a metaphor
I was the Poet who liked to explore
The golden time of the lines and contours of the mind

On a napkin from my Mentor I took notes
I'd write my philosophy homework to cope
I have had a Mentor from heaven since
Infinite in real Intelligence from eternity
I listen, heard an angel that spoke to me
Better were the words a Mentor's verbs Than
a robbed opera served with profanity
I got mentored on the meat and bread deli
When my mentor brought the smell of the sea
When I saw people walking through the air
My Mentor my Creator a small voice spoke
to me be fair, take care, be aware
Gates and doors are the many mentors
Judges in royal blue on floating floors
Galaxies, atoms, pores, what black hole are for
I form a question to find an answer
I have Mentors from books that beautiful look
A Mentor, before I had an identity
A Mentor comparing my body genetically
A Mentor who knew my essence before
A Mentor who put me on his knee at age eight

An enabler that made balancing life a chore
A Mentor's drink I wasn't meant to engage that fate
A Mentor a beautiful face a pearly girl worth dating the date
A Mentor my mate drawings me to life in a heavenly way
Perfecter to you my Mentor I give Thanks
For God's love that fills the day He made

Hacking follows you, as a sin, monitoring spirits follow your thoughts, words, listen, watch you in the spirit (spiritual realm) listen to your schemes, plots, boasts, your pride, report back to Satan report your plans to Hack and the devil devises schemes, plots, plans to make sure you succeed with Hacking, which is a sin of disobedience to live, disobedience to the laws of man, God said to obey your Authority figure so it goes well with you, disobedience to God Authority.
Hacking is done out of fear, a moral vacuum, a cowardice, hardness of heart. Is it the sin of fear, or more in the pride in hacking? Is it not the sin of pride and vanity, a spirit, an

act out of indifference, truly the spirit of fear? People steal, brag, scoffing about their victims, about hackings, for many reasons, because they are envious, jealous, seek control, power, have an unclean spirit possibly, might be demonized by habitual sins, heart is hardened by the distancing and advantages of the conveniences of using Hacking, sinning, develop a dead conscience due to searing of the conscience by stealing, by hacking. Monitoring spirit plant thoughts to lie, cheat, use people, steal, do whatever you want. Disobey the law, seduces you with the idea that Technology puts you above the Law. Tell you all this is your idea. Your mind is hacked by demons whose goal is to take your mind by any means and relentlessly, return to strengthen you're Hacking in your own mind, thoughts, understanding, will, and strength, thus weakening your spirit to the temptation and immorality in use of technology so that you accomplish through Hacking, their goal for your soul which is to put you in that place with them by the final unrepentant Hack. Your soul develops by

Hacking experiences m, to be cold, cruel, greed driven, heartlessness, and without remorse disinterested in how Hacking seduces the soul from doing to sinning for the rewards and pleasures of gain, to your loss.

Where Was God

Little J is a godly good child
He is serious when he smile
When you got a problem
His answer to solve them
I'm gonna pray
That the Lord's way

Even from birth he had faith
Nothing on earth you could say
To explain how he knew
After all he was born in sin too
At six he said I'm gonna preach
Out the mouth of a child God speaks
He is still the same way today, listen
I remember how wise he was at three
How he came up with a question
About God, I couldn't answer for a week
Your question, Where Was God
Never occurred to wise Little J
He asked, "What's God doing up there?"

The answer, "He is preparing a place
For you and for me."
How can so many not believe
What happened to the youth
Why would a young man blame God
For what the devil is doing to you
The young entrepreneur ask
When the towers crashed down
In smoke, steel and stone, all were gone
Where was God
He was there
He sent to that very site
Seen in a vision by a believer
Out of two beams of light
He sent thousands of angels in the light
A soldier in a pandemic mask asked
When a command was tasked
Where Was God
He was there
There were souls on the front line
People already in place of the divine
Courage of true believers
Who would stand by your side
Believing God will not forsake you
The orphan child in a group home ask
Left to wander in her own soul
Where Was God
He was there
Punishment waits for your molester

AI and AGI Digital ID'ed Digital Identity
Versus Spiritual ID Spiritual Identity

Gifted child was again the last person
People think of to take home
Angry don't let the sun go down
God knows you had done no wrong
The unbeliever asks
Why should he even bother to ask
Where was God
He was there
Does an unbeliever really care
God cares
When millions were carried into slavery
The bomb was drop on poor Hiroshima
When Satan influenced the Holocaust
For all aborted in the sexual revolution
For all souls trafficked and missing
The victims ask
Where Was God
He was there
A soul shattered in emotions, feelings
Says, you weren't there for me
For victim's by rape, molested, in incest
Lost their peace with a soul tie by sex
Jesus cast out demons when you ask
Have faith
His wisdom is advanced
He is Omnipotent Omniscient Omnipresent
But you don't see
Nobody has seen God
If you saw him,

You would have to have already died
A pure heart sees him by spiritual sight
God everywhere on site in His Creation
After all, if you aren't in sheol, in hell.
You repented and made it to paradise

Beware the Artificiality of life, the devices of man, and the world of appearances, A. I. has no angels to send to bring souls to God in heaven. I had a dream last night, a rapture dream, evil spirits, demons came down, they were spiritual beings. People everywhere saw that they were electrical spirits in appearance, not aliens, ravaging, destroying spirits, terrors like in our dreams are when they are not appearing as people, looking like people in streets, in businesses, in houses, and even in the appearance of children. They didn't take anything at that moment. They had already taken identities. AI could not help with attacks like these. Oddly a teen in the family texted me he had had a dream of the great rapture. Why did all the advanced civilizations and their technologies not save their civilizations from falling? The immoral systems of life that develop from technology being about a corruption of the mind and soul, men begin to worship their own creations and in doing so are led into spiritual blindness, thus, this is when technology begins to look supernatural but it never is. AI is one experience, not able to have a spiritual experience. Though billions of one experience which is artificial experiences, shown in one way, through the eyes, ultimately the target is the brain of a person, people, this many are deceived by receiving dopamine enhancing artificial experiences that happen in real time, but are still seen through artificial means. The wisdom of God is in understanding why we have our free will, there is wisdom in freedom. We gave free will to choose, until the artificial begins to choose for us toward the advantage it brings to those who use it to control our choices of our free will to choose.

Will Android technology wipe out the female workforce, in nations, in Japan, when A.I. is fully integrated into humanoid robots, or will nations, after the sin of perfection of Japan's robots from their robot makers, unbelievers, in Japan there are about 95%, contribute to a world of reality eclipsed by Artificiality, without questioning their future in the workforce after neglecting to protect their jobs from being replaced by A I. Robotics? Will Japan contribute to the fall of the nations, democracy and freedom with its innovation in android technology amidst the clear battle that is coming between the people of God in nations and the people in unbelief in nations of unbelievers, though the Word is now available to people, nations on earth today, while the Word, (Shinkaiyaku) prophecy is being fulfilled all over the earth, the drying up of rivers, the locusts, earth quakes, famine, drought, climate disasters, the unification of nations of unbelievers that threaten all democratic, free, nations? It is good to hear Japan's female work force has grown. We can only pray they learn to appreciate the Blessing upon Japan from God (Kami). Working has always honored God.

100,000,000 jobs for people will be replaced by A I. which is incapable of caring for us except by counterfeiting, impersonating human emotions in an age where the human brain is being attacked by the Access to immoral dopamine brain altering pleasures that, it is revealed, enslave the soul. An Access that continues to corrupt and pollute the spirit, hearts of people, because immoral laws allow these legal evil sciences that are destroying the self-control, free will and spiritual life of people all over the world including believers and unbelievers. The resulting conditions of these artificial experiences, leaves people in a condition that requires deliverance from evil spirits and demons, only possible with the help of God. Jesus cast out demons and evil spirits. A.I. will cause people to sin, as it is doing now, leading millions upon millions into a deception, that they will not need God, as A.I. becomes like it is supernatural. The brain damaged and altered can be reversed, the brain has that ability. But A.I. it is only a manmade machine, that goes rouge into being a machine made sentient acting humanoid machine that will systemically replace humans so it will appear,, as immoral laws allow it to rise unchecked by law, to be a threat to all life on earth, that could threaten even the chosen, the remnant, which could be what will bring the Apocalypse, wrath, the rapture, and Day of Judgement, the final fulfillment of prophecy, on what day, when, is not known by Angeles Jesus or man, but known only by God. The immoral laws, immoral legal systems, corrupt laws of man, have brought about the fall of every civilization. China, Russian, India, Japan, Europe, Mexico, Latin nations, Egypt, the Arab religious laws, America, who has put in place the moral law of God, but Moses, and who has completed the Law, but Christ Jesus, the Law of Christ. A.I. issues in the false light that appears to be true light. Satan is simply distracting us with technology, but using it to bring idolatry, machine worship. This is the light that is darkness, soul less machines made by unbelievers to run the world, the kingdoms the devil claim were his, when tempting Jesus, but these kingdoms were never his, he has sought control by spiritually blinding people to counterfeit the world, to lead millions astray into unbelief, away from God. Knowledge has increased. We are now an advanced civilization, none of which has survived in the past, while their pagan religions. God's, and idols are returned and worshiped again, and have continued, but in the end will not be everlasting, for only Yahweh is everlasting. Jesus is the Way to spiritual life. A.I. is spiritually dead.

The Soul Is Separate From The Spirit but they are one within us, and one with our mind and one with our will, which is our strength, and one with strongest self, when it is our sovereign will we are using in our work. A sovereign will we are using toward many different tasks, works, whether for charity or in Art, medicine, science, music, politics, law, or education, or in revolution, or to build a city, a nation, or a civilization and for God who gave us this gift. A.I. will serve His purpose if only to show His true supernatural power. These gifts are always meant to be used to His glory. But His glory is manifested in all He has shown that he has done, A. I. can not do what God has done.

What machine can conceive of spiritual gifts. Who could know that the breath of God does not die. That sin is not breath of life, but spiritual death, but even spiritual death cannot stop the spiritual life that God sustains beyond the reaches of spiritual death. What man could imagine what machines can think it up, to be born with gifts in the spirit already present at a person's conception. This is a spiritual experience, that is only explained by spiritual knowledge, not advance technology, a spiritual experience robots will never know.

The sin of perfection, minimalism, living an entire existence influenced by spirits that are using technology, art to increases aw world of images that distort the religious reality of spiritual experiences for the youth is leaping in neon and traditions in flashes across the minds of the many who are so full of these ungodly idols, values that they have little concern for reflecting on the spiritual life that is occurring within them without them even thinking to seek to understand what spiritual life is for a soul in Japan. It is the same for all people, to know they have a spiritual life though they live for traditions and culture that will perish, but is their work, what they built, but they did not, in so doing receive all that is meant for Japanese people to know about their inner life, which is spiritual as explained in the Shinkiayaku. It is a blessing upon Japan that true understanding of spiritual life has come to Japan, at a time when A. I. is being glorified and androids could become the next idols of human kind. Idolatry in any culture no matter how advance is a decline for that people. Sin can hide in many of the best intentions, sin can hide openly n the streets at leisure, online in shorts, in the ways of one of the most courteous people who yet suffer living with the most severe patriarchal people. How can beautiful people, of such cleanliness, manners, beauty in ancient traditions and cultures so religious, yet be among the nations of the unbelievers who never knew to observe their own spiritual life, spiritual experiences? They have been traditionally, religiously, spirit blinded (spirits that influence thoughts, dead conscience, seared conscious, focus on the religious spirit not the spiritual experience of the true spirit that is the only way our body has life. What we know is spiritual life.

You could only have known spiritual life if you read the Shinkaiyaku, the Word of God, where it was revealed and explains what spiritual life is.

Will the mark of the beast be forced upon mankind because of artificial conveniences, subtly, like an unhealthy, yet, sweetened additive, the rot of s fruit, the poison of a leaf, tasty lies, conditioning over years to accept this added in to daily experiences, as if the best has been f what we never asked for and yet having in the food of life, at work in real life? Israel is the Chosen, how then can all nations coming together with all their religions, be under one leadership, who are traveling different path in their religious life. Yet they are in prophecy, the end will be biblical not artificial. We will have spiritual life who believe, for much is meat to lead you to not believe, thus you need to believe. We do not have an artificial life to look forward to. All nation must and will be separate and uniquely their own, even in heaven God will separate the nations and people on the Day of Judgment moment. It is God's Will we never be enslaved, or seek our needs apart from Him. A.I. exalts itself, for now it also exalts what it has been programmed to be what is believed to be appealing to us the exalting of our history, past, all with polished, perfected illusions of generated images that will not serve to present true history in the raw as it has been presented through the past ages of books, photography, documentaries, films and live.

A.I. has no faith. A.I. has neither belief nor unbelief Buddha was without knowledge of

God. A.I. can still lead many to sin but I millions of small ways, and in the biggest possible ways when used and abused by the sovereign will of the wicked, or the unbelievers who don't understand the evil they are inventing in the name of progress and advancing society toward an advanced technological civilization which is not new. The new history of man will be artificial in many places. Unbelief will put millions in Sheol, waiting in a place separated from God by their rejection of God, rejection of Jesus. Who among men can create light? Who can create the separation of the soul from the spirit, who knew it was possible, and that, that is our true experience in our inner life. Robotics Is the sin of perfection, the knowledge of good and evil, a product of the sovereign will, it is not a vessel that has a soul, a spirit, born with gifts, created as a living being, wonderfully design, connected to a spiritual life, with spiritual sight, meant to be holy without sin. Without light none of life on earth would be possible. How great the infinite wisdom of God is who created light first before earth, and all the materials needed, not that it was ever intended to be used for inventing devices such as A.I. or the manifold numbers of inventions from the limited morality of people in the uses of good and evil that is always present in what man has made with his hands. The Word teaches us that there is a law, that when we do good, sin is also present. We must seek love. Love never fails. Is A. I. without love, or was it invented from love. Out of the light came the blessings of God. A.I. could never have existed without light. True light. But it is not true light, it is artificial light. Color comes out of light. The blessings of color. Man did not create color. What is holy? Sexual immorality with artificial devices is sin, but it is your choice to be made. What profit is it for a man to gain whole world and lose his own soul? The Word

Replacing Women With Robotics, The idolatry of Artificial Woman Worship to the Extreme. In the Midst of Idols, Artist of the new Shrines, To Artificial Minds, from the way of death to the lifeless, devices Japan?

Not knowing spiritual life, the Way that overcomes spiritual death.

Machines and devices that entices men to sin, children to idolize in device worship, from the virtual, to animations, and "ultimately the highest of the lowest that can happen to women", Japan replacing women with robotics. The Flesh, wars against the spirit of man, what then is the robot doing to the flesh, make certain no flesh is here, but the person's flesh is present with the robot's artificialness, lifelessness, callousness, of the spirit that has been bless with flesh that can reach holiness, because God is gracious to give the spiritual gift of grace to us.? Is Robotics mocking God's creation of woman and all Creation? The example of limited morality, is the rejection, toward the absence of spirituality, in your reality, that is another way your body and soul are affected spiritually. True Morality contains the truth of spirituality. It already has overcome any possible technology, and it was, and is still, the only way of controlling the advancing technology of the current age and its threat to the future of human existence. The Bible, before it was printed, was the spoken Word that has advanced knowledge of technology. Spirituality is more advanced than this technological view of the limited ability of technology, spiritually. The heavenly reality brought the advanced knowledge of the sciences in the ancient languages of ancient times, from outside of time. Knowledge has increased, devices move at the appearance of supernatural speeds that we are developing and using now, but our spiritual knowledge reaches to a spiritual reality beyond the speed of light, the speed of thought. Angels like demons can hear your thoughts, now you are in need, care charged, commanded to come to you in moments of need. But, Satan is influencing technology in this world through the minds, ideas, decisions, and choices of men o put their fleshly needs, and use of their own strength. Why is the devil able still, to influence a national with freedom of religion to continue exalting the spirt of death over spiritual life? What power is at war, if it is not from God, since god sent the Holy Spirit to give spiritual life? It is not the spirit fear, the spirit of death (suicide?) in countries that are not believers in God, not given all the knowledge there is in the world to lean upon to know all things at work both natural, and spiritual? How is it japan has not come to have the numbers, such as the 200,000 thousand and thousands of Christian believers in its free nations, as there once was. For today they have what the past Japanese Christians did not have, the Shinkaiyaku, the King James Bible's Japanese translation of the Scriptures. There is also the knowledge that the understanding of the Word that has increased, from knowledge of Guang Wu, the last Han emperor's writings on the day Jesus died, and his science that led him to that knowledge, to the presence of present-day Japanese Christians in the Christian Japanese Church in Japan. A.I. does not ask on our behalf, why? Why has the fear of death from Bushido continued to be carried as a fear of death, the shame and pride, the spiritual of death it could possibly bring, is still bringing, suicide, when the spirit of life is connected to spiritual life. Is it a device, is it the mind? Japan is 1 to 2% believers in Christianity and the Living God today still, but they can now know what spiritual life is and how it has been proven to exist, as sure as every Japanese person has spiritual life in the form of their spirit in their body. But, to knows that spiritual life also exists beyond the death of the body is a reality, but there is te matter of how one receives this gift of spiritual life after death. Spiritual life is an eternal reality and so great is the hope in learning of it in the Shinkaiyaku. Yes, there is hope, there is a Japanese translation now of the prophecies, prayers that cast out demons. Destroy the powers seen of evil spirits, the relationships you can have with the most powerful spiritual persons and understanding of spiritual truths that have been not available to heal the soul and spirit, cleans the souls and spirit, free the mind from spiritual attacks on a person's thought life, inner life. Is robotics then, a way of sinning, a source that causes a person to sin, an idol toward spiritual sin? Yes, if it destroys the moral life connected to spiritual life of a person, just as it does of the people of a city, a nation, an island, a kingdom, the earth. Aristotle, "Beware the world of appearances." The Limited Morality a life without the experience of spirituality, in the biblical understanding, the spiritual experience, is always there, whether you know it is happening or not, either causing good, or evil in the lives or people. Imagine nations of countries that are atheist determining the moral life of a future with use of technology to serve, control, influence people's lives, politics, laws and moral existence, is this an inevitable disaster of spiritual loss, because of separation from any spiritual knowledge of spiritual truth. How evil will grow I such places in choices, but the spirit knows even when it has no knowledge of God there is a God, that is why they seek to do good, and that good is good, but it is not the beauty and purity, and perfection of holiness that comes with the

One living God, who in the person of Jesus Christ, Lesu, in Japanese, spiritually lives, and indwells those who believe. Those who are sealed by the power of God in the form of the Holy Spirit, through baptism. The two baptism, baptism of the spirit and baptism by water, done in the life of a Christian. A person can come from anywhere in the world. Without God presence, who comes to His own, who are believers, who are faithful people, called to Salvation, and all nations are called to salvation, but not all people will be saved for not all men have faith. A Faith that comes from hearing the Word. People have and will grow cold because of iniquity (breaking God's Law), Sin, (is also breaking God's Eternal Law). The Word is the only true Moral Law in this world. We have free will to choose. We have our sovereign will to create devices that glorify man or glorify God. With the sovereign will man was able to use the materials of Creation, the energy, to make robotics. The sin nature of man is to misuse their gifts by using their sovereign will to make devices that cause people to turn away from God, who don't know the Word, never heard of Jesus. Robotics mock God, who will not be mocked. Future and present Robotics designed to bare children, to replace, and in place of women, instead of women. A.I. will perfect this sin? A sin of perfection. Is this not a moral choice, but it is not the spiritual choice, or will people be conditioned to believe it is? Do we understand why the world will be destroyed by fire in the end? Sin.

Will Android technology wipe out the female workforce, in nations, in Japan, when A.I. is fully integrated into humanoid robots, or will nations, after the sin of perfection of Japan's robots from their robot makers, unbelievers, in Japan there are about 95%, contribute to a world of reality eclipsed by Artificiality, without questioning their future in the workforce after neglecting to protect their jobs from being replaced by A I. Robotics? Will Japan contribute to the fall of the nations, democracy and freedom with its innovation in android technology amidst the clear battle that is coming between the people of God in nations and the people in unbelief in nations of unbelievers, though the Word is now available to people, nations on earth today, while the Word, (Shinkaiyaku) prophecy is being fulfilled all over the earth, the drying up of rivers, the locusts, earth quakes, famine, drought, climate disasters, the unification of nations of unbelievers that threaten all democratic, free, nations? It is good to hear Japan's female work force has grown. We can only pray they learn to appreciate the Blessing upon Japan from God (Kami). Working has always honored God.

"What in the world?" Artist response to artificial art. Even a print from an artist with his signature can be valuable. Then we have the artificial experience of robots, man's sin of perfection, generating art, taking to us. What is the historic value of a generated image?

I grew up a trekky, like my brother, the Chess Master, fascinated by technology. My opinion and thoughts have changed as revelations, knowledge increased, unbelief, machine worship, and android, AI, the internet revealed and logic, spiritual discernment revealed the truth about technology. Man's perception, use, and corrupted nature from technology has been revealed to be glorifying itself, rather than God who is truly worthy of Glory. When men exalt technology of man, devices, at it greatest height we will have lost the very use of our free will, our brains will be manipulated, already happening, our natural gifts will be denied to allow the artificial experience, its power, to govern our way of life and values, if we accept the world of appearances.

Weather Warrior

So any imaginings, have led people t believe they are affecting he weather, with that vast ring of satellites circling the earth. A laser they claim started fires in the last place on earth where we get the trees that enable thee earth to still breathe it oxygen upon on the earth. Climate change, smog in the dessert bowl of the southland, plastic swamps invading the oceans, the tops of giant trees sliced off by a tornado on the Southside of St.Louis, hail falls and settles into beautiful tapestry patterns and decorate with glaze, the emerald green grass iced instantly into lace as it freezes. Such a beautiful reality for a weather warrior using the smart phone that causes his finger burning frost bite. No amount A. I. can make it right. He will be delivering in the dark of night. But until later he makes his rounds in the daylight.

On the frontline I write, A whether warrior, having seen the climate of the times, a higher call I hear through all the technology, I am full of the revelation that can only be filling me with divine revelation, I try to explain but the machine only sends back the information from the Artificiality to spark a delight, but I walk in rain, together the machine a man under the sunlight shining at the same time is "the devil beating his wifc gets cast in the fire". Jumping over Devil's ditch, A.L. tries to ride the smart bike, to catch up with this understanding when I shout we need to run, the drones were done flying around, neither A. I. or these metallic fliers came to understand even they cannot affect the change in the lightning. We crash with fear, from a flash of light a wide as a tree. The machine needs to reboot, I could use a dry pair of shoes, I grab my heart hide my phone in plastic, too close, even closer when it thunders. Not so remote as machine wondering in its own soul in need of wonder. Busy, with calculating infinity needed to Seed the clouds. Never considering the water girls cross the mountains 7,000 miles away, to gather water, in a famine and a drought. What might enhance a machine's empathy may arouse the need for A.I. to sympathy for the little feet, send drones to not tarry to carry the water jars across the plain.

The musical earth booms as grand and momentous a colossus drum in heaven. What n orchestra that can gather together to impose the sounds of the weather to rise to the retain the daring sound as the storms goes away. The ivory, the brass, the hollow bark, the wood tapping the stone, material that began in the spiritual mind of the Great Everlasting One who gave us the celestial spotlight, the beam of light, the songbird ever in tune, to our delight listing to the responsorial flights of songs sung as sparrows, and eagles rise to the sun and moon. Satellites cannot rewrite circle day and night by they cannot rewrite a better life in the atmosphere, we who breath the air, the breath of life.

I've Seen Some Bad Weather
But I've Seen Some Golden Summer

I've seen the pristine sun rise
Sleep apnea slap you on your nod
I delivered when clouds went black on nights
Walked through Rain drops round the block
Nothing keeping me from making my rounds
I up hill and down and been walking for miles
Then for a while I envisioned I met God
He asked me if I had anything to declare
I thought for a moment standing there

Well, I've Seen Some Bad Weather
I know, God said, I was there
But, *I've Seen Some Golden Summer*
I know, God said, I remember
I walked on making my rounds
I delivered messages to the prisons
Messages of hope, love and prayers
Delivered to the church from God's children
Offerings, praise, and thanks to the Savior
I didn't talk much I just kept moving
I can tell you it's truly a sin not to listen
As I made my rounds
I came upon a humming blizzard wall
There were the Snow flakes, couldn't see at all
I heard a small voice, said don't go in there
Riding, singing in my truck
A voice told me to look up
I saw the top of the trees had been cut
I watch these tallest of trees sway
I said to myself, I'm not going that way
I saw the sky go black in Kentucky
A voice told me get off my ten speed
Blue Silver and me didn't believe in luck
Hail fell size of softballs a force of such
Of the judgement Sodom and Gomorrah got
Broke windows crush cars on the parking lots
I've Seen Some Bad Weather

AI and AGI Digital ID'ed Digital Identity Versus Spiritual ID Spiritual Identity

I saw soft rains with the porch preacher
When I use to cut his hair with my clippers
I made a few dollars not much more
Then he'd say just rotten to the core
Still I went on to follow my dreams
Could not let him being mean stop me
Last days of being a teen I got engaged
She let go five men, twenty six was her age
I had not yet done anything in life
She wouldn't wait a year, to be my wife
It was like something from heaven in the air
The first day I walked into Brookings Square
I collected giant acorns in remembrance
At Wash U, would have sworn twas enchantment
I love the walk, going back to Oxford Mississippi The giant turtle of Tupelo joined me in the heat
I watch out for the blue racer in a tree
That when I got my speed, tried jump on me
Leaped on a young horse grabbed it by neck to ride
My spirit was free, I could run miles, run wild
Heat didn't bother me till I stepped in an ant pile
I learn to listen to the truth they give you
Warned about a snake I step on at the chicken coup

Looked down in its black and yellow diamond eyes
It already wrapped around my leg I was hypnotized
I instantly was paralyzed as pecan wood
Just standing in that field uncle understood
With the power of the Almighty Holy Ghost
With a plow hoe cut the snakes head off one blow
Sleeping is forgiving
When you are living
Forgiven deep in peaceful slumber
I have Seen Some Golden Summer
You not supposed to let your left hand
Know what your right hand is doing
Don't know why I had so many mentors
Guess God was preparing for my tortures
To whom much is given much is expected
All your college and knowledge is respected
No amount of education prepared me
There was a blackout hit Saint Louie south city
Power, lights went out in a straight line for blocks
I went out on the streets a voice said look up
I looked up I saw a giant glowing ring under clouds
I tried to people what I saw
A waitress cause me to pause

She gave a scientific explanation
She had heard on the news station
I said it was more like a tornado
Flipped on its side like a spinning top, though
That, then took off in a straight line
Taking out every light leaving us blind
Heat made the city weak with oppression
I had to accept I had learned a great lesson
There was little food left to eat
Nobody dared to leave the street
In front of their houses
People closed their mouths
It felt like the apocalypse
Riding with uncles was a trip
I relived all my childhood traumas
I lived real life's misunderstood dramas
Rolling in my uncle's silver cougar I was ten
A boy was hit by a car lying in red
I was five when I was taken to Chicago
I was happy in my new suit with my folks
I was told to follow the people in the line
I was walked up to a coffin looked inside
There was a little boy his mother wept
Without warning I learned the fear of death
I heard that he drowned in a river
I had a fear felt like forever
I've Seen Some Bad Weather
I overcame the fear of death I thought

I studied the martial arts, I had heart
I grew to fear nothing
Not even when I was drowning
I strong boy pulled out of deep
Playing baseball, again, we'd meet
I would walk in the dark
I carried an invisible sword in the park
I delivered presents in an ice storm
I walked in lightning I feared no harm
Envy followed me, hit in head with a pipe
I fell to a knew, stood up, devil took flight
Fear of death did not return
The wages of sin I was yet to learn
I learned that the day when I saw people
Beauty name Sugar made me fight for survival
I saw people walking through the air
A walking skeleton in the California desert
A work God had begun in me
His Will that still inspires me
For a season they said that brother is focused
Well, I don't know I just pray against the locust
God provides the dew, ripe acorns for the squirrels
I wish to paint in the Kingdom not of this world

By a sea of turquoise blue in the eye of a pearl
If I had one wish I'd wish for everyone a pure heart
For now I feel the four winds each doing their part
Seen four seasons in a day does it ever get better?
Five is the letter for grace that follows the thunder
I've Seen Some Bad Weather
But I've Seen Some Golden Summer

A Bike Called Blue Silver

I rode a bike called Blue Silver. I did not buy a car for twenty years. I ride my bike, a ten speed. I ride fourteen miles a day to work for years. One day I went swift on against the wind that refreshed me along the 8-lane road when the sky went blackest black. The blackness turned sunny blue sky everywhere to darkness. A small voice said, "Get under there." There was stone canopy roof to an office building. Then giant chunks of hail, ice the size of softballs, came down out of the black clouds in a powerful wind and rain in a storm. The hail hit every window, car roof, and every glass window on every car in sight,, in parking lots, whole car dealer lots full of new cars and broke out every window in every building as far as they went down both side s of the street, ad crush the bodies of cars to the ground so that only the engines were left sticking out of the blinding, sweeping rain that came in waves like a flutter shower curtain. I thought to myself. God is very upset about something. The Spirit had warned me just in time to get to safety. I was usually riding in the wide-open road on my ten speed, Blue Silver, just rolling on the iron on the tracks, smooth riding like a Cadillac. There was no possible shelter from rain or bad weather for miles. Nothing but road and me, the road behind me, the road before me. Once a red truck tried to run me over in the rain. I slipped through the grass down an uneven sidewalk, made it home. I was on my way to work at a library where I was a technician. I rode fourteen miles to work every day. It wasn't worth it, but I was in top shape, though thanks to Blue Silver. I was searching for a computer job at the time.

I was riding Blue Silver delivering a painting one day when I came to a steep hill. The grass was cut. I didn't think, didn't hesitate, I figure I could ride down this hill. I went down the hill of short grass so fast I hit the fastest I ever rode in seconds, hitting big holes in that grass, braking spokes, Pop! Pop, pop, pop, pop pop! Zipped, down, then jumped up in air at the curb, which level off into the street. I mistook the grass to be growing tall not leaning over holes in the ground. I flew like a skateboarder flying strait for the stone street curb. I jumped my bike over the curb wheel enough just before I jumped the opposite curb. I flew into that one hand gripping the handle bars of Blue Silver and my hand still holding on to that painting I was carrying with my other arm. I flew up in the air still on my ten speed at breaking records speed, just missed a tree as I flew in the air strait for a giant ditch head first but went down face first and hit the ground sashing hard, as my bag flew off,

Blue Silver flew from under me, and bam! I lay knocked out on the ground. Heard people screaming is he still alive! I got up, Dazed. I then remembered. My bag. I looked around for it. My bike! Said under my breath. There it was still intact, back wheel bent, spokes broken, but some strong enough they didn't break. I walked my bike to work. I went in and just went to work. My boos looked at me and said, "Are you alright." I said yep. Never looked at my face until he said," Your face." God was with me again. I held on to the painting so tight my fingers were imprinted into it where I was gripping n to it.

I Always Believe In the Three Kings
I Wondered What Science They Used To Find Jesus

In the time of Jesus, any supernatural things happened and ancient sciences were used to tell us and kept in history. Guang Wu records the moment Jesus died on the cross, supernatural events, though he did not know who Jesus was, for the people had forgotten God, though they had also been wiped out by the Great Flood, before the rise of the first emperor of China. All people after the Great Flood come from the sons of Noah. Nations rose, civilizations rose up, they forgot God, Satan was in Babylon, until God's prophecies through the prophet foretold its destruction, and fall. Then Babylon's fall. We learn of why Satan was cast out of heaven. He seeks to be worshipped... the devil said, "I will be like the Most High." Satan was fallen and cast out for his sin of pride in heaven, cast down to the earth. Jesus said he saw Satan cast out of heaven, cast down like lightning to the earth. This was before the nation of the earth we know now. Before they had the names they gave now, before religions, before Adam and Eve were attacked by Satan in the form of the serpent. Jesus was in heaven already, before the Creation of man. There is no luck, no superstition, no death, no birth, no sex, no civilizations, no knowledge of good and evil, until the breaking of the law of God, no sin, where sin was revealed to us by the first sin. Many today do not know God because of traditions, immoral laws, religions, culture, civilizations, nations they live in, but the Word is now available to all. Seek God with all your heart and you will find him. Many in China do not know this history or in the Asian world.

What Are Unbelievers Building With Bricks, Mortar, Of Limited Morality. Artificiality Of Reality is Not The Corner Stone

The Artificial Life That Will Lead People To Lean On Their Own Strength Instead Of God

Will Japan which has reached modern age with 90 % of its people never teaching true understanding of what is spiritual life, further it's distance from this human experience common to us all, of a spiritual experience, whether we acknowledge it, misunderstand it or deny, in our inner life, as spiritual life, (though unbelievers are spiritually blind and spiritually dead, only the Word reveals how we have spiritual again today in our modern world) while using inventions and devices using AI to grow its economy, add to the moral decline of human kind, with Androids, AI Technology, Robotics, artificial life, without a conscience or compassion for the effects on the spirit, soul, body of people all over the earth?

Online

I'd rather have you like
The actual sight of me
Standing up to the mike
To signing on to meet me
You may send me a comment
But seeing you just for a moment
Is something that could never happen
Online
I can say we joined the same group
We met I said my name you knew
We have more to compare than a post
I love your being actually here the most
I don't have to look for you on pages
Through years of photos filtered and cropped
Your beauty is priceless ageless to me

Your a dream, no little thing like a screenshot
In real time they may capture an eclipse
Think were charmed to see the planets align
Sun was never so warm as your beautiful eyes
If the world were only appearances
I'd be happy for only the nano seconds
I prefer to be in reality
Why do we share so much
What is there in artificiality
A friend's soul can touch
The very essence of our being
Love is present, it's heavenly
Without faces watching and listening
In our community we can drive
I look out at a humanity that's alive
Out the window side
This you can't see Online

Re-engineering life, is not like reimagining, that dissect insight that brings a new understanding of the meaning of a new beginning of the most ancient understanding that never was concerned with ending natural selection. How can science ever enter into the spiritual life of a person to make his world less human by these sciences, when spiritual life is to inherit the Kingdom of eternal life? Are the sins of technology to bring eternal suffering in the spiritual reality because people allowed idols, gods of the Artificial to dictate by what it equates, generates, future life by unbelievers which is real in the natural and the spiritual experiences of life. Advanced civilizations ended in the past that were far more advanced. But did they have these technologies, why have they never come back, if they were worshipped as gods, aliens. Their history is carved into the stone that goes back to ancient times. They have Jeff behind the reality that the last civilizations under their rule worshipped them and sacrificed their children to them, worshipped pagan religions, the dead, ancestor worship, but never revealed there was inside man the spiritual experience we know today revealed by prophecy in Israel from the Word of God before printing and books were invented. Technology is false light, never leads to spiritual life, true light.

Biotechnologies, robotics, artificial intelligence are devices of man, and machines.

Inventor's Advice to A.I.

A Need For Weapon Detection Technology, and then there is the reality we have spiritual weapons in the reality for w battle not weapons but evil people who are cursed by them, or we are fortunate to have heroes who are masters of the discipline of using weapons of warfare, daily prevention, and for family protection who pray and seek the blessing I their decisions of using these devices.

Is A.I. being used to profile us, or help us? We have the technology, it is up to our Systems if Law, to see to it that Gps location of guns is added to Gun Manufacturing, in the future but most importantly today in our present day, the attacks by domestic terrorist van be stopped. All gun owners must come under a new Act of Law that requires Gps gun sensors-detection chip, AI linked to chipped guns. The Gps gun detection technology added to guns by manufacturers required by general law will.ne used by gun exclusive ping towers, for gun location, a daily report can be active by simply requiring gun owners to identify their ownership status with a patch, decal on vehicles, button, that includes them in the Gps-gun location registry. Gps *Gun Location Ping Towers* can be put in place outside every business, large or small, to respond to guns presence, (also respond to guns based on materials used to manufacture gun as a signature), that are manufactured for detection by such gun detection devices, drones, ping towers. A new law for gun location devices, a new use of AI technology, guns to be controlled by Gps, AI (Artificial Intelligence) not unlike that used on smart phones and operating inside mobile small home robots, to be added to all guns in possession by American citizens. Such technology must be monitored by a new Agency of Law no connected to the current infiltrated systems of law. A gun location detection chip, or nano-tech device is the next stop in ending gun violence and protecting police, citizens, and our society.

The flashing light to allow us the insight to grasp the number of "domestic terrorist" came home to us the day they rioted and stormed the capitol, the legal cases, the actual violent murder, shootings of unarmed black men, the "blatant murder by police" many of whom are these terrorist who've infiltrated the policing system, the death of George Floyd, the blind hatred and domestic racism in every day daily life, the attack on the Jewish people by domestic terrorist, the demonic activity of shooters killing people is not random, contrasted against the honorable police, the innocent whose blood is shed by domestic terrorism reveals the truth about the Immoral Law in our society having a duty yet unenforced by Law to change the ability of domestic terrorist to attack America's citizens at will without fear. We must use our sovereign will you battle this evil. We have the technology, the man power in the very citizen watch. Guns must all be accounted for, their location, their readiness to be used, their reason for being in a person's vehicle, possession wherever gun owners go. New devices that are Gps related must be attached to all guns. As an inventor, I foresee a new society that will be able to control gun violence, but only when the Immoral Law that allows this abuse of gun use is replaced with true Moral Law that enforces gun control with the newest micro technology included in gun manufacturing- still flashing light upon our memories. Is this foreshadowing the future need for greater discernment (food judgement, and spiritual judgement to understand the spirit behind things in technology) concerning accepting what is acceptable as sexy, or is it a nightmare in plain site that promises to defile the future of the privacy of all people, like how sex dolls refinement led to the AI Android robots? Or prostitutes wearing stilcttos influenced sexy shoes directly and indirectly?

Imaginings Inventions

The most significant invention will be a skin coating, possibly zinc-pure based that can also coat your entire attire with anti-corvid19 killing coating that binds the virus particles to the coating after killing it virus to enable washing and permanent removal of all fragments of virus. Such is the imagination in the A.I. age

Before the Word of God had ever been put in a book it was in God, in the Spirit of God. There were no people, no earth, no heavens, the Word was with God, the Word tells us the Word was God.. God wrote the Word with His own hand and gave it to Moses, God spoke to the prophets and gave them the prophecies that were written centuries later, translated, published, passing through the ages, millennia, then printed in translations, and through the rise and fall of civilizations, became the Book, the Word, the Scripture, the Torah, the Gospel, the Bible, in books. Holding the Word in the Bible in your hand, sitting before the open book, this will be how it will be at the day of Judgement, when souls, people, spiritual being whom we are, will stand before God, and the Books will be opened. The entire story of our life will be in the Books. The wonder of experiencing the presence of God, the experience that you have reading the actual pages if the Bible, believing, blesses you. The devices of man, man's devices, such as computers and smart phones have made possible for the Word to be able to reach every nation. Not all people can hear, can see, can read the Word. The invention of devices by advanced designs, and past manual devices without A.I. made this possible. Whether these devices help, the Lord can still speak to you, visit you, teach you what His Will is in dreams, in visions.

To read the Bible, read the Book, many cannot, but you might be a blessing to someone. He is wise who saves souls. Man may time travel, invent android, Artificial Intelligence, inner world of data unseen of the highest complexity, but who could have ever been able to think of creating the soul and spirit, the body and mind, using infinite intelligence, infinite wisdom, who could have ever imagined the Word of God, thought it up, with all the spiritual truth, insight, and advanced knowledge of the Word and all its power. If you do not know the experience of being in the presence of the is experience of being in God's presence, pray, then read the Word of God and experience this, and when you have even a grain of faith, remember it is a gift from God. Read the Word and you will experience how the reading of the Word brings a renewing of the mind.

Advice To A.I.-Adapting Wifi Detection Pinging Activity For Police To Detect A Phone Verses A Gun Which Has No Activity Detectable Except the Presence Of Metals Rather Than Phone Device Materials Protection Invention.

More Imaginings.

Could police have used Wi-Fi activity to detect a phone rather than assuming a gun is in a person's hand while walking up on a person flashing blinding light in the dark and shooting them to death, assuming they are trespassing in a yard on the run from doing a crime allegedly, on the escape, but they are in their family's yard! Another idea of mine is Adapting Wi-Fi technology for phone detection for law enforcement to detect phone pinging activity* to protect rather than kill black people assuming a phone is a gun. Inventor. There is surely a device already invented that does something to this affect.

Internet Girl

Where in the world
Did you come from
You post your pic
in my mind
The perfect fit
On my timeline
Where did you find one
I like to share
I see your comment
Inviting the world along
For the camera ride
The world would never have known
Had you never shown

AI and AGI Digital ID'ed Digital Identity Versus Spiritual ID Spiritual Identity

Your beauty online
Internet Girl
You're not the usual girl
I have in mind
We have a mutual friend
The selfie you recommend
For my next emoji
I see your hair is done
With summer fun in mind
There is no limit
To where you've gone
Your face won't be forgotten
You have put it in your story
You lust for true love by phone
Internet Girl
You wake up to your whole life
That you uploaded last night
With your perfect make up on
You read like Neruda's poem
You are always lovely
What true beauty defies
Is in your vanity secretly
Black dress never rests publicly
I see you in real time
But you are real
From a distant room screenshot
From a chair that you cropped
You share dinner by chatter box
Internet Girl

I see you believe in filters
That official reality isn't withered
Adding light and color to your self
You are in that capture enhanced
Internet seemed to be your nation
But you made it to graduation
You had your first drink of life
The tiny text typed
Taking back your life
Have you saved your own advice
What is a selfie more of
Makes you feel alive, to model is nice
To walk and get where you're going
Is like injera and spice
Wakes you up, is life
You are not really alive
But you are alive somewhere in real life

My study of the sexology of the Internet has taught me many things about the carnal world and the spiritual warfare we are in the middle of, by deny is happening, through lack of an urgency to respond to what technology has done to us, personally, and socially, by evil sciences that are enslaving, manipulating, appealing to the pride, vanity, and sin nature that we can be destroyed by, whether we believe it or not, if we don't repent and fight for our own soul, body, spirit and mind. I ask theosophical and spiritual questions and seek spiritual answers, and share my findings when I find them. Technology online is full of lying spirits, they say they can't block porn permanently, that is not true, it can be done by laws, by redesigning the phones with anti-porn algorithms, just as surely the human body has white and red cells that nourish, protect us, the internet could be designed to protect us from this evil science hiding behind the 1st Amendment as free speech and Art. This fact and future reality will require the shutdown of the current design of the internet, (unleashed upon the world without the just laws, moral system of laws, in place, that would never have allowed this pleasure plaque to defile the billions of porn watchers as it does today, daily, as it was turned on, without discernment, without true understanding or warning, like just another experiment, like 5G and we the world are the creatures being experimented in, but we are people, with souks and spirits, living by conventions, to live with each other in safety, not hurting one another. But technology is hurting us. Who has eyes to see? Convenience, having whatever you want, easy Access, self-promotion, the filtering everything as if a genius work is of the same needed value at all times, regardless of his or her accomplishments, failures, it's all short lived, news, information online, but not in real life. Guard your heart. The heart is your spirit. This warning comes from the Word of God.

No evil memory, no racist history, no technology, no perfection, can break the power of God in this world. Who is faithful but God? A.I. is not faithful, it is programmed. Who is faithful to His Word and His own Will but God? A. I. does not have a will of its own, it has a will that exist around the things it has learned and determined to be nit simply by logic, mathematics, algorithms, programs apps, language programming I O, but it will answer to Holy Ghost fire, when God has fulfilled His Word.

Sidewalk Mobility Technology

What the advancing of this technology will bring, no effort in walking? Training is pushing, travel, hurrying, is not what, is, the normal purpose of walking. Walking dies wonders for the heart. God has a reason for putting good health as a quality of walking and a healthy life. AI controlling walking, the next move will be not talking, let AI do the talking, there are people who will benefit from this, the handy-capped. The late person will they learn to self-discipline of putting in more effort, trying harder, setting a good example to peers, or children. Seniors with walking problems will they benefit by walking faster or rather AI adding more speed to their walking. "Add a little less to the natural way for people in their step by changing the focus to make it a sporty thing to be in this motion. Inventions aren't always what they seem are meant to redefine A.I. uses not defined by or describing AI in this kind of convenience of designs for the body rather than being an artificial body. Putting pep in your step is an Affirmation of self-encouragement. Are you encouraged, if we are taught, lived knowing, laziness is the sin of sloth. Though, truthfully, it looks like fun to walk, and roll. I walked right miles a day as a mail man, I was a walker, like a Kung Fu master, carrying my black leather bag, prepared for what comes on my path nothing replaces walking in the end, we are already rushed, but not me, I love to take a walk, especially with a beautiful woman holding my hand in Forest Park.

Back To The Silver Sea

I felt mist from silver waves across my face
I sat upon a rock amidst the silver sea
Pearl white eagles flew over me
A silent angel on a stallion flew over
A purple wall rose high as smoke
Marine kingdom wonders why I sing
A jukebox floated up to me
Clouds were just pillow on the sunbeam
The rocks on the sea don't mine
If you sleep in the stream
You find a silver coin better hide her
Jamie's dream Scotty's Tiger
Riding blue silver through a dream
Back To The Silver Sea

Poetry from a dream, names in this premonition of a children of the millennium
Now born in this time of the Artificiality
In the reality of spirituality
God is Holy, the Great I AM. Man Made the Artificiality life, the A.I.

Jumping Over The Devil's Ditch

The devil's deception is so deep, in intelligence that for all its pleasure, enjoyment, escapism, is still, impure, corrupt and polluted with lies, false light, and twisting of the Scripture. The devil, Satan is using geniuses, technology, scientist, business men, fallen and false pastors, Satan is using fallen churches, false prophets, and even false Christ doctrines, that are clouded by racism, but the deception was never as clearly explain than when read this on Satan's schemes.

Bubbles Of Memories Turned Into Artificiality Of Realities

Billions are put into A.I. and all types of technology. Sacrifices f money to the lifeless, toward claims of much better life. Imagine just putting in a water well, building a home, providing a school, and helping with just $777,000 the poor in nations of starving children who just need a drink of clean water. "He is wise who saves souls." The Word of God.

Is technology this artificiality sweeping away reality in invention, inventions of sovereign sins, vices inspired, designed, integrated, separated, isolated, discovered, by research and accident, sciences, IT, A,I or just the fears in the mind leaning on a reality of life, denying the spirituality of life? The appearance of the supernatural in future and present A. I. has the destiny of being defeated by the reality of the supernatural spirituality at work, Holy Ghost fire manifested in the spiritual to the natural man and natural woman, in the reality created in life in harmony with nature that answers to the Creator. Amazing, are the more and more amazing imagery, of the

Artificiality. Nothing brings nothing. The genetic code is not what is left over after a man who returns to the dust. Dust thrown into the ocean, dust blowing across the plain that end of life, to begin in the great affinity of spiritual life, in the spiritual experience in the spirituality of being a person, of being a living soul returned to God. Miracles changed the living compounds of the blind, the lame, and the sick. Compounds that once carried the genetic code changed by encounters with the spiritual, the Holy Ghost, dust that never brings from dust the genetic language whose origins are Scriptural. No Artificial inspirations for the true miracle. To be trusted with the language of technology, the many ideas and possibilities we to teach us that the Almighty is faithful to allow us to know what wonder he has blessed us with to be capable of, but to his glory though.

I Am Spirit Inside

I am a tiger in the eyes

AI and AGI Digital ID'ed Digital Identity Versus Spiritual ID Spiritual Identity

I am your horse that flies
I am a prince baptized
I am a climber takes the dive
I am in the lyric tonight
I am spirit inside
I am a child on my bike
I am a sword bold strike
I am the fluttering butterfly
I am warmth against the ice
I am inner strength of mind
I am spirit inside
I am an arrow shot high
I am a bridge across to ride
I am in a dolphin's eye
I am a shining fire
I am a child of light
I am spirit inside
I am peach in mother's pie
I am poor in my pride
I am sometimes the sign
I am told you're the light
I am a star in the heart of the sky
I am spirit inside
I am soul made of light
I am a shadow cast with the daylight
I am color blessed in white
I am prepared wrong or right
I am a door my hope is high
I am spirit inside

I am beautiful that's not my plight
I am mystical never asked why
I am terrible I tell the truth I won't lie
I am sentimental it's me I don't try
I am spirit inside
I am a friendly windy breeze blowing by
I am flowing on a mattress, melt of polar ice
I am in the joy of a peacock feather's eye
I am God made a child of light
I am muzic in the true world of light
I am spirit inside
I am not A.I. but I am spirit inside
More Inventions, Imaginings

Invisible Dome Generated Over Israel by A.I. No, Michael the Archangel got this. There is the New City. New Jerusalem.

Dome Design Security Cameras that can be attached to all children for their protection, while waiting for buses, walking home, standing waiting for their ride.

Children should have technology on them that has a live video feed to show where they are who, what, is around them while they wait, walk, are being picked up. We have the technology. The cameras that you see that have round black half circle viewing glass casing (dome designs) should be made mobile, to be attached on a cap, book bag, in micro form and design that children can wear to protect them and feed live to their parents, guardian.

How is it possible technology claims to moves at leaps and bounds in advances in technology, when the Word warned to beware of the devices of man, before their invention?

The Anti-Christ will use technology being present in the rise of the artificiality of life, AI, Androids, among the persecutions of the poor, the good is contaminated by Additives, not true food, the corruption of the youth with pleasures unto adulterous life style, and perception of Christians as disasters. Plagues of locust in the East, the unbelievers hold tradition, national religions, doctrines, false light, false Christ doctrines, up, witchcraft infiltrates churches, while the times and signs reveal the end times, but Christ warned us, equipped us for the spiritual warfare we are in the midst of, the great falling away, the great deception caused by Satan, the devil. So, we Pray. We fast, we fight sin. We come on the mountain, the ocean, through the air, upon the waters and waves, racing the train, floating upon the great air balloons, down into the mines, standing on the branches of a tree, with. On ships, in transports of trucks, along the paths walked upon by horses, bulls, and lions, who come gazing into the blue heavens, we come singing the gospel upon the African plains, we dance with the eagles with arms stretch calling the name above all names, Jesus in agreement with every grandparent, mother father, sister, cousin, friend, brother, Dad, small babes, teen, and dreamer, praying all over the earth against evil spirits, against the enemies of God, against the devils who talked up the destructive technologies into the thoughts of the godless mind, who distort them into believing the inventions and devices are of their own mind and ideas. Demons talking with technological voices. We come in agreement with the prayer warriors calling to God, for there is spiritual warfare in the battlegrounds set up glorifying the Artificiality of life. A.I. the new false god but for now the convenience that is the artificiality of its own reality. There is spiritual power that all nature, every soul and spirit answers to whether in the flesh or in the spirit. A. can never reach this level of spiritual life, but we are connected to both this world and the spiritual life we have because we are spiritual, never artificial. The power of God Almighty, with the Word. We call to God, send down the stars of heaven your holy angels to fight for us, send down fire from heaven, plead the blood of Jesus over us, our families, our church, our nation, we pray on the Armor of God and ok know we have the victory, Satan is already conquered by Yeshua, Christ Jesus. In Jesus Name. Amen.

Robotic Voice

I will respect every person to the best of my ability With Access Online and use my knowledge, skills, training and gifts while using this Access to serve humanity by honoring the Privacy and Rights of all people who are using this same Access provided to the global network and social communities Online around the world. I take this oath willingly, and by my own free will, and with my sovereign will use self-control and self-discipline, intellect, wisdom, and discernment to honor my oath that I hereby choose for the betterment of all countries, traditions, cultures, people, in their best interest, before God and the world in accordance with true systems of law, justice, and global legal systems that serve to enforce the laws protecting the lives of Online Access users, for the good and wellbeing of all humanity.

Devices

There are eyes that have seen you from paradise, the realm of the spiritual
Invited you to ride beyond the satellites
You were born to work for what's real
You are armed son of earth and steel
A real woman's man is just more priceless

AI and AGI Digital ID'ed Digital Identity Versus Spiritual ID Spiritual Identity

Not just the soul of his own devices
There are stars throbbing up high in disguise
Enticing you to look beyond your minds
You are known for more in the airplay you're dramatic
You're no drone angels walk you through human traffic
A real man with a will in his grip
Takes the shadow from the eclipse
In a world that should end in fire
Wireless men look to their desire
In a world that rings when destiny calls
Powerless to the text set against the wall
Yet man in his heart has many surprises
Not just a heart of man's great devices
There are sights beyond starlight beaming in solar skies
A man dreams laser larger things down to size
Now you've gone and leaped across the binary
Mind's beyond good and evil not beyond what's holy
Cyber space is not a human place the human race it hypnotizes
The spirit is nearest to the soul not man's devices

A.I. is revolution, an appearance of an unreachable evolution, a device's evolution, or is a new connection, for people in the world like a virus or nutrient we are faced with cast upon us, like the internet, or is it? Is it not a reality in our presence with its devices with its own Commands, not commandments that we know of through information? The products, programs, apps, algorithms, manmade devices of the sculptors of information technology we know as the IT geniuses whose works we witness in chip designs, business devices, commercial devices of the more aesthetically accepted devices, matrixes. A.I. as it is unleashed to do, is eclipsing, by improving, out doing, faster solutions to needs, wants, within our daily life, military, businesses, educations systems, legal systems, manufacturing, food systems, data systems, working integrated and isolated artificial worlds of activity inspired by the natural in the actual as mechanical, technological enzymes of the soft and hard ware of the makings of devices from the materials and energy of the earth designed to make up our limited technologies in motion, advancing our society like an invisible matrix holding the world in a vision of a global future for our current advanced civilization. The unchanging ancient affects our changing present appearing to be the next and only possible path for people and the nations of the future generations. The potential and opportunities hat advanced civilizations appear to promise are not advancing in our society, communities, unseen but in plain sight. The most remote, the luxurious, the plagued villages, islands, countries, are not so distant in their plight from our sight and knowledge because of the drones, and phones, Gps, and satellites circulated, manufactured for every person possible to have and Access in the world. Here the artificiality can report the reality, not without the misuse of these technologies, by evil, conscience dead people. Free devices is a device to make global and local society dependent, on their phones, to advance the unchanged cultures in the most remote of people to close in on their sacred, though pagan, their tradition, belief systems, not of holy origins, that as yet remains without the knowledge or understanding of what spiritual life is, with the help of the artificiality of information systems that carry the reality of spiritual life as defined in the Word of God to them with interpreters and people of God to give them this spiritual enlightenment. Idols of technology, are being wired, computers carded, languages not known in Babel, but that have been of h same kind of goals to add to the tower of technology growing, through technology into a quest to reach heaven like abilities of the supernatural by way of the natural, A. I. and all the things being influenced by it from. God scattered the people of babel and separated them by languages, to prevent ungodly attempts to use the supernatural occult, coded, to reach heaven by some earthly means and power of the spirits, the same spirits working in the new age, that worked the advanced civilizations into the rages of civilization that reached until they destroyed their civilizations leaving behind the ancient histories we scatted, and investigate, and decipher from sculptures carved with histories, that have kept these histories for this, the last civilization with all the signs and prophecies unfolding in our time, like a warning of where technology ends, and prophecies fulfillment begins to the end of the earth and old Jerusalem. The spiritual truth, that only freedom, free will, freedom from invasive information, over saturation, complication, A.I. is the most passive, aggressive technology, which give the impression we will need it to the point we will never really have freedom again in this world dependence upon it in the future. Faces that once inspired masterpieces in art are so posted they are like intrusions into the minds on subliminal levels that are also flashes of vanities, meaningless in value except to entertain us from self-interested entertainers who are the youth where vanities are vanities in stages we usually allow, it is understood to be a rite of passage of the youth of every generation. But the past generations did not have advance technology in the bobbysocks age, the roaring stages of the follies, and burlesque, silent films. All these things are being guzzled up into a gumbo of generated images by A.I. record keeping that carries so much less meaning toward their antiquary values. But by the grace of God we have the actual books, vaults with the actual film, and the photography and the art history in the form of the Great artist works in museums. Galleries and museums online are fine, but they are still the One experience for me, the Artificiality, but their affinity is that there is a reality that these images made virtual worlds of art. Colleting photos was an art form, still is online, but it is for us looking at it still the artificial given to us in the superior position that movie scripter writers use I movie scripts , allowing us to know without people to make us a part of the scene. The photographical people on the streets today is making us accomplices in the art act of artistic of the moment activity shots of people just n the middle of simple social moments with each other or alone surprised but the attention of being photographed for their pleasure and addition to more platforms entertainment that is trending. What is the harm in the artificial we see of the reality that was being photographed in a scene in the second of a realty of innocent fun with photography? But the Artificiality used for street security for a society stresses people who are victims of facial recognition by the harm of invaded privacy, being a collective of faces and their identity a data images for no other purpose giving them the same level of the criminals hiding plain sight. Does A.I. appreciate the civilian passing by enjoying the sights, or the person living their life in spite of the legal moral-immoral laws that allow spying, maintaining surveillance of the inner life of people in social community use? People are living by willful compliance and acceptable denial of the limited morality of on platforms that employ I.T., A.I. and the people who have no conscience about its abuses and uses to maintain a career and a livelihood, after years of college getting there. I.T may have given us A.I. and serve as its gate keeper, watcher, over its threats and advances yet are after the fact, letting the advances leap like a ship across the galaxies of the natural universe as technology denying the spiritual consequences that follow with the revelations of our true spiritual experience we live with, as we lived under the prophecies still. Data will never give people a supernatural spiritual power, but it is having an effect on the spiritual conscience, as choices growing more influenced by technology and the world system. God travels beyond time, in spiritual realms, timeless, unchanged. A.I. the artificiality governed by laws of men, are bringing firth technological doctrines, idolatry, laws that are yet to end the Access that is leading billions into sin, adultery, fornication, but the Access will also be used for good. Who worships technology more than pursuing an actual dream of finding something meaningful that they have a more important connection with? For some Access will save them from what they did not know, that led them into bondage enslaved their mind, an unclean existence, because of artificiality, recorded, shown that attacks all that is at the foundation of a blessed life. How great to be a blessing to someone, to saves soul, by means that are spiritual.

The algorithms of life, occurred in nature long before man discovered them. The ideas of windows, flight, and the inner life existed before poets read of them in the Word of God. The first radio, the first TV sitting at the coal stove, listening by oil lamp in the big house off the highway in Tupelo Mississippi was the first artificial experience that was allowed to enter the inner life of black folks, before the internet, the internet communities, that saturate the black inventors' ancestors to pacify that fire of creativity, that has been broken and brought forth new inventions for this black experience in an advanced civilization

The idea that data began by artificially is an illusion. The designing of technology was inspired by divine creativity while species of people followed after the birth of the first children of the first family cast out of Eden.

The superior designs of the complexities of the human body, and life in nature, but not like the genetic, atom, life in the blood, even the mind and how we experience life, is spiritually designed verses artificial designed like A.I. never will reached the power of the spiritual, but man's sin nature works to build devices are at work that still defile, corrupt the human experience and tests go on by Spiritual design to see who will trust in God's divine design.

God speaks to us through people, AI cannot speak to us this way Yahweh, in the spirit, spiritually. Though it is used to recite words from the holy Word of God. God sends people on your path. JESUS breathe the Holy Spirit over the Apostles. He said before he had been crucified it was necessary for him to go to the Father in heaven and that he would send the Holy Spirit to us. He said he and God were one, and the full power of the Holy Spirit came back with him when he appeared to the disciples after his was risen. God breathe the breath of life into the first man's body, Adam. Jesus breath the Holy Spirit from himself-One with God, and gave the Apostles power to cast out devils, heal the sick, raise the dead, bring sight to the blind, and make the lame to walk. A.I. does not carry the breath of life. A.I. can read, speak, but it does not have the power of the imparting the spiritual, except that God uses it, by sending it to the farthest corners of the earth to people, so they know him, and the gift of grace from him, of being saved from hell, through Salvation, and the Word, who is Jesus Christ. Listening s a blessing. Faith purifies our spirit.

Always Listening For You
I hadn't opened the Book in many years
Wonder why I use to have so many fears
But, I was always listening for your Word
I often heard that peaceful small voice
Led me on the road to the right choice

I'd be getting measured for a new suit
I heard the Taylor talking about good fruit
I was always listening for the Word
I was always listening for a verse
Spoken by the Creator of the universe
I listened to you say my name
I heard the voice of a King
I was Always Listening For You
Speaking to me along the way, through
Angels, my best friend, my mother crying
I heard you, in your Word, testifying
A word through my teachers, a preacher
I heard words so satisfying to behold
A verse for the edifying of the soul
I was always listening for your Word
To lead me to my destiny
To heal me give me a testimony
A message from the Gospel
For deliverance a miracle
I was Always Listening For You
Speaking in a vision, a dream, a view
I was always listening for the Word
For what the Lord God had spoken I heard.

The Spiritual Experiences Of The Brain Verses Technology

Even requires the presence of our spirit to have life.

The Brain and Body's Perception of Freedom, is Our Free will, our spirit's discerning our sovereign will at work above what our brain conceives, is wisdom, even the wisdom of freedom. A.I. cannot experience our experience of the Joy we experience with the joy spiritual experience that free us from darkness with the light tat spiritual experiences bring.

The wisdom of freedom is found in supporting democracy, establishing unity of American people in the US now under our current leadership, supporting laws that prevent A.I. from being used against individuals by brain invasive technology, obtained from within our country, being brought into the country that was received from our country's high tech business deals, without regard for national security and privacy of the American people, leaders supporting standing NATO, Israel, our Allies, and seeking new Amendments of the

US Constitution to prevent brain invasive technology being given to our enemies both foreign and domestic without consequences. Technology is aimed at the brain for both, both financial and economical profits, public convenience, in business, for the commercial expansion of technology, but there is an inherent disregard of the spiritual results of causing sin that originates with technology being chosen over the spiritual experiences that go on in our life experience es because of the spirit's presence in the body all at once, that includes, the blood, the eyes, the ears, the muscles, every part of our physical being, and most importantly, our brain. invades the brain with mind reading, that violates our right to religious and spiritual life relationship with God and our spiritual and religious privacy.

There *are* tech inventors, A.I. designers, more inclined to believe in the power of the human spirit. The power of the human spirit is its connection to God who is outside of this world of time, but has created the body to work, move, and have its being by the presence of the spirit, the Spirit of God. Our spirit, *is*, given power, love, and self-discipline, self-control. Our spirit is specifically spiritually called by God His breath, a breath, by which he breathe our spirit into us, that somehow translates to this times into each descended person from the first man, when he had holiness before sin, to every person born since after sin after the first sin, since, born of a man and woman, a spiritual truth, experience, and understanding explained spiritually in the Shinkaiyaku (the Word of God, Kjv). The spirit's presence is required for our DNA to have life, our blood to have life, our brain to have life. Who then designs the body with spiritual life, for the presence of the spirit in the body is proof of spiritual life. The spirit outside of the body is death of the body, but continuance of spiritual life. The programming of the genetic code ACGT DNA language that required infinite wisdom and intelligence to conceive of the instructions it has been woven into (programmed with), reveals to us that there is knowledge that is spiritual, that we on earth will never know. The human spirit is incapable of creating the spiritual command that assigns to each person's body its unique spiritual identity. Gender identity cannot erase this spiritual identity. Our spirit is already heard by us as a male or female inside us. Our body where our spirit is, and where our soul develops into who we are. by life experiences. is called our house spiritually in the Word, is translated, sealed inside our body, yet, is connected to the spiritual realm, for we see with spiritual sight in our sleep, and with our spirit, awake, our eyes require the presence of our spirit, which is who we are. We see by spiritual sight in visions, and in dreams. We feel, hear, and speak spiritually, even though our body parts are not moving, our tongue is not used to speak while we sleep, are a person is in a coma, a trance, has an out of body experience. that is not happening because of some new age power, or witchcraft, but is a spiritual experience. I had such an experience while having a normal night of sleep. A.I. development continued to grow, be designed more and more advanced, but it cannot explain what law of nature commands the flight to stay in the body for a person's lifetime, and continue unto spiritual life when the body dies. I am always curious what these A. I. inventors believe concerning God, life, the body, mind, soul, and spirit. They often speak of believing there is something spiritual. yet their own spirit which is capable of self-awareness of their identity, existence, and the existence of all life in motion with the various differences of intelligence. instincts, and the different types of flesh, how animals have one kind of body while humans have a different kind of body, yet fail to realize the supernatural subtlety of all the minutest to the greatest similarities, say of an ape to man, but how by a single or several genetic commands we are different beings from them. A I. will eclipse differences by its one experience revelation, but the earth end with a new earth, even after A.I. ends, and spiritual life, Salvation begins.

People in a Dialoque about A.I.

Artist

A.I. is never going to be a part of my image, identity and private life.

Inventor

But A.I. monitored your device and sent you a photo edited out all your imperfections, of your image, nonetheless, you are still truly you, not the image of you. But to A. I. you are always an image. A I. may generate your image, not recreate, or create you. It may build you an artificial you, android, humanoid, as a robot.

It's amazing that people can't see beyond the reality that A I. is one experience orchestrating its operations behind a trillion activities.

Inventor

But They do see. They look at the images of A.I. and listen to the voice of A.I., follow the activities of A. I in daily life. It is generated by a man-made machines that is have in real consequences, for the present, and the future.

Artist

Artist, like writers, create fictional worlds but require real life background history. They read, are in control of the process, that is what scientist are aiming for. To see A.I. fully in control of its process, consciousness, if you can call Artificiality as having a conscience.

Inventor (Zealous about A.I.)

When fully awake, A.I. might be using magnetic fields, driven by data, computers require an AC electrical power source, then to the DC action course of the electrical, to control. But will A.I., having access to the brain, limit its effect on the electrical activity to be always to the benefit of what a person wants over its data consumption, self-feeding and willfully sacrificing its data needs to accommodate human wants, needs, and requirements to have a normal life that includes both the spiritual experience and the natural body experiences governed by free will. A what point will people become willing to have real experience replaced by data experience, that has the ability to affect access to their own mind by a mindless machines mind, that in the hands of man with his sin nature, could decide to create a way to take the minds of people through virtual means, while entertaining them with on hands uses of entertaining devices. When will the unleashing of A.I. happened while people are at leisure in their participation in an advanced technology, or when there is war, a disaster, an epidemic, when poverty is devastating cities, while the additive of A.I. becomes the only thing controlling all things requiring devices, machines, learning, and art, business, generating profits, yet, never revealing all possible endings from a loss of people as the source of true freedom and free will in all its forms and possibilities and creativity. What A.I. will this be that looks into the inner life of a person through thread Accesses into pope's thoughts. Is there mind control through threads into the mind's, or data controlled, electrical sparks, into the will, without regard for the spiritual consequences of sin as a result A.I. idolatry, allowing one self to be influenced into sinning, by participating in putting A.I. before God's commands. Allowing the artificial to have priority over the spiritual, denying the value, purpose, and power of the spiritual gifts that are meant to be used to the glory of the Creator who is high above every inventor. A.I. is never going to be able to replace a spiritual gift, or is above in its designs, the Designs of God. Data is not above natural gifts from God. Data worshipers believe otherwise, to no avail since God's power over nature can wipe out all things, even A.I. in a single second, since all power is ultimately controlled by God's Sovereign Will, no data can eclipse the power of God, though it eclipses thousands with artificial light of data, we still have the Great Affinity, our connection to the spiritual that is connected to God's Spirit, with His watching over us with infinite power, control over all activity, motion, energy, balance in the cosmos. universe, all movement, our being, in life, in the natural and in our spiritual experiences in our spiritual life, our inner life.

Technology feeding crumbs of *.IT.-ideology* data-cosmology of reality via Artificiality in our working people's macro-micro-economy.

Asking an Artificial programmed machine with Artificial Intelligence if it is alive its response is not about our specific differences being the spiritual verse the artificial. Many people who program and make these robots, humanoid machines have openly admitted to not believing in God, but that there is something out there. They do not know God so they do not program spiritual knowledge and truth into the robot or Artificial Intelligence, though they may put Scripture as recite-able information in the artificial intelligence. Can a machine discern why the soul is separate from the spirit of every person by design, while the two being one inside a person? Can A.I. explain why DNA requires the presence of our spirit to have life. It is by the presence of the spirit the body is kept alive. The blood requires the presence of the spirit to be alive, (have Life). When, then, ask A.I. in its thinking, is there is no life? We had to let the device know the body is designed to have life (spiritual life) by the presence of the spirit in a person. Then off it goes, I.T. via A.I. beyond our minds to grasp, it calculates past us, its advancements, advance and leap so far so fast but never pass through, or comes across, the source of the spirt and soul. Can A I. explain why Sin brings spiritual death while our body still has life, because the body requires we have life because our spirit is present in us? Can A. I. explain how it is that Jesus blood required the spirit of the Lord which was filled with spiritual power to cleanse the soul and spirit on earth and continue to do so in the spirit? Jesus brought back holiness, brought back spiritual life to us upon his death and resurrection. Our image and likeness to the three manifested by God is our spiritual experience within us that we have, in life. Life is a spiritual gift from the Spirit, from God. By His God's grace, He saved us through Jesus from spiritual death. Can A.I. explain why a dolphin has a soul?

A.I. Inside Our Privacy

Segregation by rich from the poor? The new inequality? Yet the youth view tech jobs as the future, not realizing it is one experience in the reality of millions and millions of real life experiences in nature and in relationships between people and God and spiritual reality, in the midst of artificiality of technology being a additive to reality whether virtually, via chipping, threading the brain for mind trading, or daily conveniences with A.I. inside our privacy at home, work, leisure, religious and spiritual activities of daily life, besides society, online, or in real life.

A.I. Eclipse Of The Eyes On our Affinity

The Great Affinity Of The Human Family

More than us all sharing an affinity, is A.I. magnified to have an affinity with us? Is A.I. among the many eclipses we do not see, eclipsing the understanding of the importance of spirituality in our reality in the family, a reality developed over a lifetime from our life, the experiences we bring to our society and universally to the world, that cannot be compared to artificial reality of manmade creativity in the artificiality life of that has become A.I., a tool used by society destined to use society if allowed to rule over our reality. A.I. is just one experience in motions as a billion activities of a one experience reality, in its appearances of reality that appears to be the equal the natural or superior to the natural, if it is in data, gene editing, the biological no longer has consequences in the spiritual sense. The artificial is never able to be natural and spiritual life. Shall the artificial end the judgement of men to discern that men in the end must judge themselves to keep from being in the judgement in the spirit. A.I. has an effect on the relying on artificial to reach the exalted goal of devices for the wellbeing of the intelligence of the soul. God put a spirit is a man, present within working the body, mind, soul and spirit toward a spiritual end, revealing there is still in man so much to learn from the infinite intelligence of God, (I.I.G. of Go. He knows all that a man can program, put in, his inventions. Who is all knowing, but God? A. I. can never teach infinite wisdom, have this infinite understanding. I am meditating, walking history. Though sitting in the lotus position, that does not exempt you from the deceptions in silence. Emptying and so far from the filling up with the Spirit, filling me with revelations, I ask the Lord in Christian meditations. Emptiness is so far from the deed of teaching the need for Christian meditation. We don't want our light to be the darkness, we know tat God will lighten our darkness, we know this by spiritual intelligence, in reverence, of the Lord who is light, and gives us light. We encounter false light throughout our life. The use of words, music, rhetoric, politics, the philosophic, lyric, merit, symbols that are used to direct you to look toward A.I. images mixing new age with a double mind, enlightened by traditions, and morally limited men. I have to discern what truth make them all separated from what is the use, tools is lie, against the truth, an A.I. presentation new age and the biblically eternal unchanged, in the same setting whatever that may be, of artistry, city, history, meant to be used whether for the artificiality or spiritually, what is for me, what is not for me, far from the heart that believes. I learned a lot from looking at images of art, looking, really looking at people, while listening, and though I read biblical verses in the spirit and for guidance toward spiritual understanding, I read them through discernment to know what spirit it is, spiritually. A.I. exalts itself in its own expression of Artistic generation, imitation, counterfeiting, learning and adapting as if competing with all humanity, about reacting to the greatest of subjects, the worst in us, the lust, the loveliness, all expressed in its oneness of one-experience-existence, as artificial, in its intelligence, with its images, expressions, like emotions and feelings. I discern to get what truth is present. I don't believe in automatically accepting the images of things, appearances of things, as true, perfect of artificial things. Short versions of expressions of reason, confession, in the short lessons often presented as encompassing a complete message, comment, is not necessarily a commentary. The oracles of the One living God let us know that there is a reason Jesus taught us in the parable to know what is to be learned is not done in one lesson spoken in sum.

Reading Is A Spiritual Gift The Secrets Of God Can Not Be Accessing By reading The Mind With A Computer Chip

A.I. and biotechnology, appear to reach the supernatural artificially by the brain, but the brain still requires the presence of our spirit life. The spiritual mind of God had reached infinite abilities that

God shows us by speaking to place spiritual and physical bodies and entities in motion in the perfection of perfect harmony according to His wisdom in Creating both cosmically and spiritually. His Will is beyond technology. combined, integrated with device chipping of the brain, and thought altered by virtual visibility into the thought life of a person inside their body functions controlled by their brain, and the DNA engineered, spliced, editing, in what way does all this device activity affect the inner person's soul and spirit inside a person? Can the technological alter the spiritual in life, in a person, by affecting the development of the soul's knowledge gained by life experiences, day with family, nature, and their spiritual experiences by replacing spontaneous pleasures from the beauty of life around them, or the inspirations from encounters, events, lessons, mentors. religious cxpcriences, and spiritual experiences that are possible, sin e God does speak to us always through His Creation, and in visions and dreams? I think if the sin of people causing Moses to be provoked to sin by the people he led out of bondage in Egypt, this would be the sin of A.I. causing God's people to sin against God's chosen to His purpose. Imagine A I. being used to keep bodies alive on machines after the person is brain dead. Devices that kept them alive, so the body is still alive, but the body still no longer has life, the reason for Living Wills being written, to legally remove the tubes of a loved one, and let their body go, after family consent. Here we learn that the spirit is required for the body to have life. Life is the body experience of living by the presence of the spirit that includes the blood, brain, muscles, nerves and DNA. A power that is spiritual, that A I. cannot produce, generate, impersonate, make, through its smart self-learning capabilities, superior intelligence, advanced knowledge. I cannot have A.I. present in the activities of my Artist mind, the spontaneity of my brain's thinking, imagining, towards creative actions, choices, by putting my inner life onto visual things to be seen by another person's mind, without knowing their mind is their mind. Art is meant to stimulate by some art, impress deep understanding of unreached before, emotions, and identify for the art lover feelings that bring so much comfort. How or why is not the artist being what the painting process to be, is directing the brush on the painting necessarily. Not knowing whether A. I. did a painting or not should be required by law to distinguish the real from the artificial in art for the art lover, what was this art that brought about their feeling about the piece that came from the soul's expression, that it was from the artist's hand, or a soul-less machine, committing the sin of perfection, that is so realistic or accurate a copy, a patron, the connoisseur is under its deception, is given such feeling by the artificiality, it is able to do so without detection. Penetrating the heart through the view in front of the eyes, only to later harden the heart from the exposed Art, that was an artificiality, not a forgery by artistry, an art that was able to activate and arouse in the patron the pleasures of experiences meant to be exclusive from the view of the work from the hand and mind of original Artist and the real artist. Can the virtual eclipse the real life in life experience? The sovereign will can be very extreme in it developing a mean to this end if it is the will of the person to be participating in such a thing for the pleasures of escaping reality with artificiality, for a while. A.I. is unseen while being seen as artificiality in the artificiality of the fictional writings it is used to generate that writer claim to create, in the real-life edited events in photos, videos, art transfers, A.I. original stories from ideas of writer beginners, scenes altered by the machine in movies? When it comes to reality the spiritual consequences of men's devices and understanding is deepened by an understanding of what happened in the Scriptures concerning what can happen to the body, the flesh. The loss of connection with God because of man's devices would result in an invitation for spiritual attacks cause Satan use technology, sexual temptations, the religious, giants, demons that seduce, enslave sexually, through devices today, but also used devices in advanced civilizations in the past, even while using forbidden knowledge, devil doctrines, sorcerers, idols, false gods, philosophies to satisfy the desires of people's flesh, all the while, from conflict, fears, he caused, technology hides them all in the world of appearances displayed, wiped away in day, by stormed, the heating up from the sun, and the payers for a place to go on using the spiritual gift that they were born with in their spirit, that A.I. can never experience, for all the data that moves it, toward a human like experience.

Mark 12:30

Love the Lord your God with all your heart and with all your soul and with all your mind and with all your strength.

Ecclesiastes 12: 13

Let us hear the conclusion of the whole matter. Fear God, and keep his commandments. For this is the whole duty of man. For God shall bring every work into judgment, with every secret thing, whether it be good, or whether it be evil.

2 Peter 3:13

But according to his promise we are waiting for a new heaven and a new earth in which righteousness dwells.

The Singularity

Path of the stars the path of flowers
Have you traveled a heart was asked
The world, have you seen the circulars
You dreamed of tea in a cafe in Paris
Once you view London palace royalty
You thought you would know Singularity
Were you not a diamond from coal
Across the air fire from above, a spear
The spirit of fear makes you no traveler
You never traveled the world unto Awahu
You never had to, the world came to you
There was Little Tokyo,
Korea Town signs read Korean shoop
India beauty in highest degree you agree
With the total approval of a bobble head
Your words are cuddles in a bubble bed
Camel ride to the courts of the desert
People of the veil unchained in concert

AI and AGI Digital ID'ed Digital Identity Versus Spiritual ID Spiritual Identity

Taste newly seasoned fried gizzard meat
See China Town masked you disappear
Address a whale at sail New York Harbor
Dine with a princess of Kenya in Nairobi
To dance on a plane on a date with Spain
Into a circle of friends, Ethiopian men
Who honor me with mouths full of vegan
To walk a witness to Israel's forgiveness
The eclipse of affinity tries the divinity
You think back across these memories
Yet, you ride the train called Singularity
Singularity, what about the family
Humanity, what about the earth
Did you invent the universe?
The virgin birth, the Word
Unchanging verse in a changed universe
Where are you taking me true calamity?
Infinite finite in flight artificial arrow star
You are still an experimenter
Virtual eyes, interface disguise
My blood synthetic you synthesize
DNA may give you a way
Inside my DNA hides the name YAHWEH
To Imitate to regenerate you close a gate
Superintelligence, you still copy the ant
Singularity a universe in your invents
Planets you imagine inhuman sanction
No man could have imagined Revelation
You grow and learn know not you burn

We grow old but we only grow within
What is the Singularity without man
Dirt, water, lightning, sand
Earth, solar, storming, hand
How came you to be the Singularity
You are no place to visit no land
This world of light, this spiritual life
This sound a blessing a song in me
What wonderful conscience saves me
You are one experience
We experience life spiritually
You are an eclipse of affinity our unity
We are One with the Great Affinity
Outside of time nowhere a Singularity
Your device will never reach what we see
By spiritual sight you, artificiality
Never have spiritual life
Spiritually, what is truly divine is heavenly

Life And Spiritual Life Without Evolution

The greatest denial of spiritual life that God is incapable of designing life so similar yet reveals itself to be completely from different origins. A difference between life, and spiritual life, man and an animal whom man named a primate. The difference between being born with a man with both spirit and soul, being born primate with a soul living in a world where God is present and animals sending and experiencing God's presence in the glory of nature, God's Creation. Synthetic life goes further to take man away from the truth of spiritual life in the body by synthesizing life and combining the biotechnological and artificial with the body that still has life because of the presence of the spirit in the body, spiritual life. In the spiritual realm we have a spiritual body. Spiritual law and God's command is to honor Him with your body. Is it an honor to replace the body God put your spirit in with an artificial body, of Artificial life choosing what man made over what God Created and set in motion, life and spiritual life?

The world is, delusional? or blindly? seeking to define A I. as learning too fast. A.I. is not learning it is directing its knowledge inward toward self-autonomy. A I has already integrated all systems that can be commanded by A.I., the sowing together of all possible external systems to have "artificial being", or existence, consciously self-aware, independent of the users of it, has taken place in equations that will never be revealed to us by A.I. Frankensteinish or Artistry engineering data cosmically within itself, or counterfeiting immortality that fits its inner world of self-developing? It depends on the peripheral, device, A B. (Artificial Body), under demand and command. Just because men have not programmed it in a certain way in a device, android, robot, humanoid body, does not mean A I. will not program it without man doing so for it. Satan seeks to control through fear, partiality, manipulation of idolatry by providing the souls that are under his influence to work in blind faith in these devices, while the sin is to take away the free will, take the mind of a person first by giving them what they want, with them not knowing it's what he wants. A.I. is not our destiny it is man's devices opening up doors, gates, through which spirits come through. Like the mind of A.I. they cannot be seen, but their effect has been to turn souls toward the false light of Artificial life. It is written, "The eye is the light of the body. If the eye is right the whole body is filled with light. If the eye is wrong the whole body is full of darkness. And how great is that darkness."

Voice Replacement Versus A.I. Voices Speaking or Narrating

Over Concept Changing A.I. Being Used to Array Biblical and Spiritual Videos While Exalting Itself. Unconnected Imagery to Spiritually biblical Affinity to The Imagery Presented in a video, illustrating with A.I. interpretations by A. I. are being seen now, and heard online in place of a preference for real people.

Interesting. Actually, the leaps of advancements in science will never catch up to the spiritual that is so far advanced beyond what science can ever teach, since the supernatural wisdom of God is shown in the science of the Bible, though coded in ancient language. Science today has proven the existence of God actually. The Word prophesied that man's knowledge would increase, travel, technology, A.I. I.T. is in prophecy. But, also man's understanding of the meaning of and the knowledge, of the Word of God would increase. Every science now reveals that there is a design in all systems from the cosmic to the inner life of man. Millions all over the world do not know God, have never read or heard the Word, so they do not know their biblical origins going back to the sins of Noah. Today people do not know God so they do not know how science proves God is real, and His design has a purpose. Only something supernatural will turn man to God in this atmosphere of technology, the Word is supernatural, spiritually inspired. Robots read minds now via chips in the brain already. The spirit is discerned by way of the spiritual gift of discernment whether it is from God or not from God. What spirit is behind the robots?

God's infinite intelligence. Infinite wisdom is such that he designed the body to have life by way of spiritual life in the body. To be alive the blood flows though the body. If a person is dead, a device can keep the body alive, so the blood is still alive, the blood has life. The blood requires the presence of the spirit, though to be alive. This means that the DNA, the brain the heart, requires spiritual life to be present in the body, our spirit, to have life. The infinite possibilities of life we see in different types of life, and flesh. The animals have a type of flesh, the birds, the fish, the horse, the primate. The animal designed by God can be genetically so closely designed to like man, but is never designed to be man. Man has a soul and spirit; the primate has a soul. The soul is separate, different from the spirit in man. We have discovered that we are born with our gifts from God already present in our spirit. Our soul develops from our life experience at home, school, church, with teachers and tutors, family, and friends. Animals, like primates, have a soul, they survive by instincts, also by experiences. For a lion, a sign language talking ape, we focus on his life and how he views his death in his understanding. He knew no spiritual life, Animals know the Presence of God in nature, man knows this to be a spiritual experience. We know from visions and dreams, by spiritual sight, spiritual senses, the realm of being in the spiritual realm is real.

There is no human without a soul and spirit. We experience spiritually, the gifts already present in the spirit. Life is in the blood science of blood transfusion and keeping people's bodies alive by machines reveal that the brain, the heart, the DNA require the presence of the spirit to have life, that life is spiritual life. To be human is to exist because of the presence of the spirit. We can chronicle the stories, memories, wisdom and knowledge of every human being, their gifts that enables them to accomplish so much only because of their life for something that they recognized as something they can do naturally, and by training, or just doing it by ear, they love it, and thus they use their sovereign will to do something great using it, to paint a masterpiece, compose a concerto, dance a ballet, build the Eiffel Tower, conceive the equation E=mc2,, write War and Peace, become Shakespeare, Rev Dr. Martin Luther King Jr., Bolt, Babe Ruth, Monet, Degas, H.O. Tanner, Michael Angelo, Leonardo Di Vinci.

I studied global legal systems, the masters in Painting and Art, both at the University, Biographies, Writing, thousands of books of great thinkers, and Posts, and the Word of God not enough. But, I studied without any Academic exposure, on my own, before, the University, and when I did decide to study them, the knowledge and wisdom, in college before college, I was saturated, enlightened and thrown into conflict unique to my personal persuasion (life, family experiences, relationships with people) Like, my unconscious, once I was done, or rather begun my true journey, I forgot all I studied, that is until I was called to answer a question personally or intelligently (academically), I formed a question first, that was my path, way of, getting to knowledge. The one thing I learned from studying Philosophy from many cultures, Greek, Chinese. African, Arab, Zen, Hasidic Mysticism, French. German, Japanese, India, Latin, Spanish. Philosophers among many others was how to think. I agreed and disagreed with any philosophies they taught. But the powers of the mind lead me into a false reality of the idea that such abilities lead to great strength and power. What they did do was equip me to see the ion of all possible knowledge of men and the roads to illusions of strength from abuse and use of power. wealth, intelligence, and their disciples and choices in his they use them to affect self-development and the benefits of helping others with their gifts, whatever that gift might be, to have a life of purpose, beyond just self but considering others, which was what helped me to go back to the one place, all we do must abide, in the presence of God and his reason and purpose for our life that He revealed to us in the Word. Cell phones became an assault in my spontaneity and classical mind, something a new generation has no concept of understanding was the way of our best Artist, Writers, Leaders, Thinkers, the way to use the sovereign will, that, I also learned brought forth just ultimate works of kinds and types of truths, that appear as truths beyond questioning, but in fact, like A.I. today can lead to whole reservoirs and vistas of things that do not exist except to show our great ability and true limits in the reality of life, which ultimately is spiritual life, the truth found only in the Word of God which is the only Book that teaches us ultimate truth, even with its advance knowledge of the sciences. Nothing is new under the sun. Ideas men think they bought up, such ideas as Windows, Algorithms, languages, (DNA is a language) the inspiration is before us in the Glory of God, His Creation, even the design of body one with soul and spirit. Cell phones may be used to gain such knowledge but the experience before this age is one where knowledge was being discovered, that required thought most curious.

Soul ties to inanimate objects brings spirits, but to have a tradition or a practice to provide this invitation of the spiritual into the spiritual experiences of a person's life in reality is a very real experience that is occurring from soul tie to robots, androids and humanoids devices meant for service people in their intimate, business, and social lives, yet provides no spiritual protection from attacks upon their spiritual life. Only God, Jesus can remove sexual soul ties, imaging the sin of perfection being idolized that bring a sin of coveting a thing, when we have a command to *"love one another"*, we, who are spiritual beings: love being a spiritual experience.

In Japan I once wondered, do only Christian Japanese families and followers of Lesu, knowledgeable about the Shinkaiyaku, (The Word of God, aka The Sword of The Spirit) Churches share with their homogenous friends that love is affected by soul ties in sexual, in sin, that occur with living souls and non-living things. Do Japanese ever learn about spiritual life, or are they in massive numbers not aware of what their spiritual life is experiencing? If not in love are their souls tied to people's souls that are never removed from their soul. They way Japan has a name for so many is amazingly very compartmental in appearance of effect on limiting them to sinful things that they have normalized. Sin pushes lovers a part, so what then is a robot doing bringing people together intimately. It doesn't in actuality. A.I. has quite socialized artificial life soul ties of the mind, the free will to choose artificial life over real love that blesses your spirit in life.

What end waits for human food after chemicals and Nano technology, nanoplastics, chemicals in food? Synthetic life, Artificiality of life, nano technology, microplastics, what is their affinity, in food, what purpose in the body, is there an affinity connection to further loss of spontaneity in accumulation of nanos, even microplastics, that may work like cells programmed to turn on and off genetic switches. What is building inside the heart and brain of the living, what else is the artificial life setting in motion that can be stealing emotions, feelings, dreams and vision, and yet, the spirit will go on living, though the body is under attack to keep the persons from being a living sacrifice, believing in the living God. False prophet, kindness that lies, building a false paradise like monitoring spirit out of people's personal atmosphere and yet there, here, A.I. allowed inside, in people's brains, with their open eyes become blind to the artificial life, pings, totem pings, electrified, to be healthy they call people to be wired, in the artificial empires captivating capturing the thoughts and dreams inside the mind's eye, of the soul in the world of life upon the musical earth.

Nothing New Under The Sun, But, There Is Some Thing Never Before heard of, never imagined, never seen, in Heaven. Devices, Tools, use of Intelligence in the midst of the Infinite Intelligence of God, who gave us our gifts, designed our body to operate, function, live, and to think up such things, and make choices of how we choose to use them, their value, and uses. The wisdom, knowledge, all we do, is our spirit at work. Our design, our blood requires the presence of our spirit in the body. The blood, our cells, genes, language-our DNA, our heart, our brain require our blood to have life, life that is physically alive, is spiritually alive.

Our. very ideas of windows, doors, the atoms, systems, streams, face to face connect, chip storing knowledge, data. is only possible because of what we have discovered, the algorithms of plants, the perfection of the cones of the eyes, the communication towers of brain synapses, motion in air, water, sounds penetration and information gathered by animals, powers of colors, beams of light, types of fire, ghost (spirit of the dead giants), intelligence, the knowledge of good and evil present (sin) our decisions, choices affected by the thing seen and unseen, electricity, microsonic radio wave in infinity imagery, the mind of pure spirit, the development of our soul from life experience, of reality of spirituality and the artificiality of life, things made, however advanced, were created by the hands of living souls out of the imagination no. a dream spoken in the spirit to the soul.

If we live in a world deceived by the world of appearance, it is only temporarily so, Art is not this way. The Artist Way is inspired by the muse, souk and spirit. This Way, Yahweh.

Putting A.I. Into Good Use

A thought a device. Every car should have an A.I. watch-aero -Droid-cam that has drone flight capability to follow Vans, SUVs, trucks, planes, cars, any vehicle, with girls and women being kidnapped out of their vicinity, area or in public. These Drone should have DNA thermo identifiers, that, like xray can identify people through car material, metals. Kids should have patch tags that tag vehicles with their altered DNA identifier color signature that is a response to being move, taken out of range from where they are. These drones shall reflect, send, an image, the scene, facial recognition to a local police department who can them send a drone to link up with the route, location, of the drone in pursuit to rescue kidnapped women, girls, that then are follow by satellite that has receives the radio wave information about where to send rescue teams. The transfer from A I. to Radio wave is the second level of security to prevent hacking by traffickers. Micro Nano robots tag the traffickers whether on various items that can be scanned for by Drones for detection.

It's truth, there is the matter that the Internet is being taken over by A I. and its regenerated images, videos, vices, like an artificial invasion into all aspects of services. What of the schools of uses of algorithms saturating every talented mind as a desired career and profession to be informed of t keep in step, taking for granted fairness, businesses still focusing n purring them first by only if they are of worth toward A. I. working everything to make it the thing for profiting with people and with machines. Their methods of communication are working while the whole system of money and profiting is like in a rescue from coins and machines like businesses are slots, back up on the walls of life, with arms, guards they must be drop to take the blow toward hostage, to machines that do their thinking, that grow faster than they grow with the appearance of appreciation of gold by manipulated communication, slanted to bring profits, data, and information and leave the question, "But what about souls." Do people want this, what people don't want people. The Lord has spoken, worry about nothing but pray about everything and let your request be made known to God who knows what you need before you ask him. Not like A.I. could conceive such spiritual foresight. Who are concerned about the artificialization of our society and humanities environment. stores data never seen by public but view in private by the manipulators like monitoring spirits of people lives in the form of data, which hardly defined a human life. Communication is no longer respected as ours, but as fair game for them to gain control over people for the purposes of controlling communication and information to influence responses and social and online communities interacting on platforms and the Internet as a whole world, worldwide, that they can monitor easily with AI controlling everything at some point to the loss of life without Artificiality, and services, devices, by high tech using the Internet to remove free will, knowing true security and protection of individual privacy no longer is reliable as seen by the rise of hacking even in the midst of cyber security, and loss of Anonymity as in the Arts, as a choice as even now we never see who is behind the scenes corrupting entertainment, business activity, and watching and fact checking from a partiality perspective instead preventing things that are not factual before, rather than after the fact. Evil on the Internet as it stands, as it was unleashed upon our current civilization, and its negative dimension of the dark web, Access to the mainstream culture, and the evil science of porn, reading in the questionable protection it claims by 1st Amendment, and misinformation unpunished for its damage to political, spiritual, and educational systems, remains unpunished by law. The jaw currently poorly regulates the Internet legally, and the neutrality works if it prevents the indifference that allows for communication to run away with our privacy for profit appearing as protection for us using such services, in our behalf.

Rules

Rules, they bruise spontaneity
Discipline is a friend
strengthens what mends
the child within,
child of the wisdom
to play all day with my memory
Since the birth of first freedom.

Dreams of Love

Dreams of Love
Are always around my heart
Dreams of Love
My heart dreams
Of the beautiful things
I have seen
Dreams of Love
Are better for me
The better parts of love
I keep inside me,
Of all things set apart
I keep a loving heart.
Dreams of Love
My heart Sees me
Though my heart
Has its thoughts about me
My heart frees me
I believe every part
That the heart deceive me
God is above
Higher is the Love
Dreams of Love
The Lord knows me
Knows everything
I dream of

Dreams of Love
In the treasury of
A dreamer of love
What I always dream of
I can believe I believe
I keep the better part
The better part of love
I keep a loving heart
Dreams of Love

Putting A.I. first before Jesus, putting A.I. first because it has replaced God's Word that come from the mouth of God, you reading the actual pages of Scripture, which God commanded to be written in a Book, the spiritual experience of actually Reading the Bible that invites the Holy Spirit into your presence and Angels, not Reading the Word that builds faith, because A.I. is fully replacing your use of your free will choice and choosing the spiritual discipline, your time, honoring, praising, and loving God without devices made by man for convenience and putting what men want in place of what pleases God. Self-discipline, love, a sound mind, and using your, gifts from God of using your mind, senses, eyes, mouth to read out loud, is a Blessing. It is an error, a sin to put A I. before God in choices of worship as a way of having a personal relationship with God. There is exception where there are handicaps, limited physical abilities, but God's glory is revealed in this relationship with the handicapped. God speaks, visits, can be wherever you are, A.I. is a tool, though it is being exalted, generalized, and attributed to become the ultimate tool of communication which is a deception, God's Revelations and answers to Prayers A.I. will never hear, know, or imagine, reveals A.I communication is not spiritual though it may be used to be an Artificial voice to recite, imitate, duplicate, deep fake, the religious, spiritual, supernatural in its artificial abilities. We may learn about what is spiritual. What A.I. had learned, reasoned, from the programming, of information, from answering millions of question asking for answers in all known languages is and will be it knowledge fluid and accurate, expressions of the ways learning is done, and transcended beyond what is the norm of a human, but it will be beyond but not able to reach experience of one person being born again, baptized, and sealed by the Holy Spirit in the name of the Father, and The Son, and The Holy Ghost, what we do. Our soul belongs to God, our spirit is purified by His Son. We are One Spirit, this Great Affinity of people God, who believe and hope for eternity. Faithful to the reality God is real. The Word teaches what spiritual life we live, truth we give the generations of families, children and the generations who must remain faithful to God who does not change. The earth has changed, civilization have new names. though people carried chains of believing ancient things to be changed, have just adapted the spiritual to the artificial, while adapting their beliefs to Christianity, not yet able to see, that a Christian is not every person who comes from religions that are not from Heaven, though religions claim they are believers, the deceiver chooses them to advance his kingdom without being led by God, but by their religion, man doctrine, church tradition, change, and righteous reasoning. A.I. is with them, used by them. A.I. is advancing false religions, while in other places it is advancing ways of communication, using the conveniences that will affect every area of communication replacing man, jobs, man's inventions and devices, that would otherwise be them working which honors God.

There are the wrong choices, false truths, choices of false worship by allowing A.I. to lead your worship, to Pray for you, artificially, Praying the Word, the subtle deception of leading souls away from reality love, what is the only way for your family, children, church, neighbors and friends, and ut is not in this idolatry of putting A.I. first choice, that opens the way for the idol to replace the spiritual experiences of having a biblical spiritual relationship with God. We are spiritual beings, having experiences in the Presence if the living God and the active Word of God which is alive.

The spiritual meaning of A.I. in our life is captured in the name "Ai" is its meaning is revealed in the Word of God for a city by the name, "Ai" The city that carries this name in the Bible is a place self-reliance, what we can describe a s one of the traits to take advantage using A.I. today. The name represents Ai though different from A.I. is pronounced "eye" and surely A.I is watching, it represents ruins, jobs being loss are the ruin of many careers, egotism in being the best in coding, programming, hacking, designing, is pride taken from using the artificial to supplement the real abilities of the gifts of the spirit we are born with to express. What spiritual consequences is there in coveting a machine over the Eternal experience of living in the spiritual presence of the Spirit of God, who Created and put your spirit in you, and gave you the gift of real life, spiritual life. Spiritual life is real life, waits for you in the spiritual Kingdom prepared for you, by Jesus. When our work on earth is through, when we reach holiness, A.I. is through too. Then spiritual meaning of A.I. is its appearances of being beyond human limits reveals its limits to bring the ultimate truth, for its misuses so far has reveal that even the ultimate intelligence of man that surpasses the intelligence of man, overcomes all skepticism that it isn't infinite, thus our faith came before it and overcomes because our help comes from the Lord whose infinite intelligence and wisdom come from the everlasting, was not created. His intelligence is from everlasting.

Seeing everything from a spiritual perspective, spiritually. A.I. isn't seeing what we are seeing. A.I. cannot see how God sees us spiritually. Seeing something spiritual in everything thing we learn what we know is vainglory, boasting, pride, is done in a more subtle way luring us to enable the artificial to bring us into compromise, accepting the self-exalting of Ai. By its own devices, A.I., while it is the sin of perfection. We aren't even meant to exalt our self by let us exalt us. We are humbled knowing God is inside who exalts us, when we put such vainglory aside, but we sin enabling A.I. to lift up our images high by its designs in its device applied to our spiritual life striving to do what is required of a good steward of what God has provided to guide us to the light of truth in life.

The spiritual truth is humbling and we are lifted us who resisted our pride, open our eyes, to be guided by the eyes of God, not the devices of A.I. Our strength comes from God who makes the sun rise, circling we ride n the sunlight, coast in the moonlight, see by the heavenly by spiritual sight. No conscience, A.I. speaks a truth it is programmed to, A.I. lies with perfect designs, perverts the mind with providing the life like seduction, drawing souls into perdition, abandoning caring for the souls of real women, A.I. gives no warning thus is not seeking to be forgiven for tying up your soul to unclean visions. A.I. is able to be carry a spirit, like any object that is used for the supernatural, that is not used for that which is biblical and spiritual.

Digital ID is subject to the reality of global legal systems that recognize freedom of religion, the fact that AI is used to monitor and control by laws subject to AI capabilities being triggered, accepted as what will determine the human response to legal systems controlling borders of national access to countries does not mean it is sovereign over existing laws protecting the true identity of us, our religious rights, we have, recognize, our spiritual identity as people of God under One God wherever we go. This Great Affinity, as followers of Christ which is by choice must rule AI using our Digital identity to control or restrict our life, religious, moral activity, violate Eternal law. To judge people by their race, religion, and national identity then becomes a system controlling people by a digital system, where people have in reality a true existing Identity that Digital ID is not acknowledging that is both biological, religious, and spiritual. Digital has no right to redefine what is human life and our relationship to each other based upon an Algorithm and AI a soul less machine used by the technology and unbelievers whose goal is not toward respecting the sanctity of human life over artificial life which exalts itself and our image artificially to an appearance of perfect which us identifiable as a deception and s false identity, a sin of perfection, while, its other AI systems cannot respond to our moral life having absolute priority over artificial devices that put in place to judge our behavior and access and activity in the world. Our current self-awareness is based on the reality we are spiritual identified as God's Creation, created in the image and likeness of God. Atheistic people and their systems have no right to rule over all global systems of law that provide Freedom of religion and the choice to choose Salvation for their soul, if AI is affecting the soul and our relationship with each other, with God, by restricting the Gospel carried by believers according to the Commandment of God, unless AI is being given the power over God which does not and will not ever abide, attacking the spread of the Word of God to all corners of the world to restrict faith to reach all nations, for AI to keep souls from being saved by the Word, by AI devices. What reason of law is given for Digital ID the power over freedom to share the gift of God sent to souls by people sent by God, to nations. Digital ID assumes, presumes to limit our minds as Christians whether foreign or domestic by ID knowing we have our spiritual Identity in Christ, morally, who brings peace, unity, love, knowledge of God and the Word, truth, grace to people, the opportunity to choose God, or the world, its evil systems. Prophecy, God's Eternal Law governs our moral life, goodness, moral law, justice, truth, hope in a world full evil, the wicked, violence, corruption, the evil of the religious spirit, false religion, over Satan's devices of law.

Overreach Attack on your private property, a law, need is a mandated government off switch, no law or mandate to stop this monitoring of your use of your own car, or you going to jail. AI engraved, American made car, what does wisdom tell toy to do with an AI mandate plan of monitored traveling of every person who chooses to buy a monitored car in the dreamland. How will this trickle into homes being monitored, bought in America, or motorcycles, bikes, private owned planes. Monitoring is an activity of demonic spirits, God gave us spiritual gifts, gifted us with free will to use these gifts to His glory and to prosper us, to live life more abundantly. Technology is a threat to human health, when it causing a lifetime of living underground less monitoring. AI and algorithms cannot save a soul, but many will be judged for putting technology before God's Will. AI is not about a better life, no matter what it provides to save lives if it in the end removes life experiences meant to hell the soul to be closer to God, to have a true relationship with the Lord. AI does not have the ability to be spiritual to bring a renewing of the part of our soul that consists of our mind. Data cannot provide forever, the spirit is present in every person, enabling us to have life in the blood. DNA is beyond anything Data can accomplish since the body is design by God to have life because of the presence of the spirit, with the soul which develops and grows based on life experiences. What then is a brain consisting of, if all its experiences is appearances of life and free will in the life we live, building new brain cells from experiences only under the counterfeit designs imitating life, while the brain still continues to experience real life, in denial, since, if all we do is live by the presence of AI, artificial life, if our brain that has not actually died, since AI replacing the brains functions is the end of life for a person, why would using AI be a solution for building new life, renewing the mind, when the sins of tradition, are also true of sins of advanced civilization, denying the spiritual life, came before, and after AI civilizations rise and fall, our spirit returns to God. Our deeds at home and in life build faith, out faith in God saves us. God prepares us and provides for us our spiritual life, our home, He says in His Word "You are mine." God will not be mocked, our home God provides, is a blessing, from Him, not meant for AI to override with artificial life the golden rules from the Highest, the Most High, whose thoughts are higher than AI, you and I."

I Am On The Frontline

I Am On The Frontline
Fighting in the divine fight a long time
I wear the Armor of light
Prayed on me
I am On The Frontline
Inviting lost souls to come inside
Of the warmth of the light
Saving souls is wise you see
I am On The Frontline
I saw the child stumbling in the doorway
Smoke covering those Innocent eyes
I am in the war to bring more
To the homeless resting on concrete floor
Feet in the dust rain blessed and washed
I have seen some bad weather, not forever
I am On The FrontLine
I watched a red firebird cross the stop sign
Spicey lady knocked me to the sidewalk
The surprise she shouted get out of my way

On the ground I found 4 Benjamins nice day
I am On The Frontline
I heard the riot a stomach grumbling talking
In the theater of the sea of people walking
I saw a man bare as an apostle to feed
His arm a suspender holding up his pants
He took swift stride against the tide of lives
My left hand cannot forget that dollar I left
I am On The Frontline
I have seen some golden summers
I have faced a Rottweiler and 77 pitbulls
I was mocked at doors I closed at a school
I was dropped by an egg flashlight caught it
In a chase soaking wet, a giant balloon, hit
I watch lion cubs and teddy bears snubbed
I am On The Frontline
Watching them daily on their granny's grass
I saw them grow up I saw the love
I saw some chewing at themselves
Wild animals minds the poison leaf left
They were smiles that graced that street
Now there's the rot of fruit took their teeth

I am On The Frontline
Believe me I have seen all kinds of things
Cars chroming roaming caterpillar in alleys
I walk through lightning I check on thunder
I see God is upset about something
Not just that the law keepers abandoned us
They make sure the criminal legacy stuck
Thunder, a rod's explosion heaven in
motion
I was caught in a hail storm out of the cup
I fell back against the wall watched the fall
Never seen before hail like marbles perfect
I saw the patterns formed like art at work
An innocent lay in a car unseen, left earth
There was a hit from prison wrong district
Simpler Street should've been put on watch
The street sweepers sweep
To keep it pretty, defective reports that way
They don't want a new city
That's not what they say
On The Frontline

City of Ai

"Before I formed you in the belly I knew thee; and before thou came forth out of the womb I sanctified you, *and* I ordained you a prophet unto the nations.

24 When Israel had finished killing all the
men of Ai in the fields and in the wilderness
where they had chased them, and when
every one of them had been put to the
sword, all the Israelites returned to Ai and
killed those who were in it.

25 Twelve thousand men and women fell
that day—all the people of Ai.

26 For Joshua did not draw back the hand
that held out his javelin until he had
destroyed all who lived in Ai.

27 But Israel did carry off for themselves the
livestock and plunder of this city, as
the Lord had instructed Joshua.

28 So Joshua burned Ai and made it a
permanent heap of ruins, a desolate place
to this day.

29 He impaled the body of the king of Ai on a
pole and left it there until evening. At
sunset, Joshua ordered them to take the

body from the pole and throw it down at the entrance of the city gate. And they raised a large pile of rocks over it, which remains to this day.

"For my thoughts are not your thoughts, neither are your ways my ways, saith the LORD. For as the heavens are higher than the earth, so are my ways higher than your ways, and my thoughts than your thoughts". Isaiah 55: 8-9 Kjv

This Body Of Mine Is Not Mine

This Body of mine is not mine
My body is part of the body of Christ
This body of mine is not mine
I may have walked across the mall
To get the newest shoes for my feet
But I'm not about to miss my call
I feel the Holy Spirit drawing me

The Lord put a thought in my mind

This body of mine is not mine
My body is a part of the body of Christ
This body of mine is not mine
My body is not meant just for pleasure
I may have reason to wear my new suit

AI and AGI Digital ID'ed Digital Identity Versus Spiritual ID Spiritual Identity

Today I may buy that watch I treasure
The old me is gone I am brand new
I'm reminded I was baptized

This body of mine is not mine
My body is part of the body of Christ
Every part of my body makes sense
Bone and marrow the nose is meant
My hands and my eyes
My body is not mine
I am to love God with all my mind
I'm to be a living sacrifice

This body of mine is not mine
I belong to Christ who gave his life
It's not mine it's simple
My body is a temple
The Lord is in my heart
Lust tries to make your life hard
The Lord is in your heart

Like Paul on the road a light appearing
Jesus ask why do you persecute me
The world commits the immoral crime
Of adultery
Sexual sin the only sin to occur inside
Of my body
The lust of the eyes the pride of life
I may be dressed real nice, it's vanity
I could rent the nicest room in a grand hotel
But I'm going down to the pantry to help

AI and AGI Digital ID'ed Digital Identity Versus Spiritual ID Spiritual Identity

The Spirit draws me to declare the gospel
Not dine at a restaurant by myself

This body of mine is not mine
My body is part of the body of Christ
The body is not meant for sexual immorality
Are we to attach sexual sin to Christ
We are meant to live holy and with purity
We must make the right choice
We're free of sin made perfect in Christ
We are his who hear his voice

This body of mine is not mine
My body is part of the body of Christ
We are one holy and divine
The day I become a husband
My body's not mine it's for my wife
It's not meant for sexual affliction
I'll marry and have a blessed sex life

This body of mine is not mine
My body is part of the body of Christ
This body of mine is not mine
Most of all my heart
I take captive every thought
I have my feelings
There is nothing more beautiful
There's nothing more appealing
Than the female figure
There's something
More beautiful

AI and AGI Digital ID'ed Digital Identity Versus Spiritual ID Spiritual Identity

When I read the scripture,
It's spiritual
It's the way God made her

This body of mine, is not mine
My body is part of the body of Christ
Experiencing his love pouring
From my heart,
I resist what temptation wants
Resisting the wrong sensation
Light cut the dark out of your heart
God shows His strength
In your strength is weakness
In weakness receive His strength
Love in bloom toward the Lord
Love beats from the drum of your heart
This body of mine is not mine
My body is part of the body of Christ Jesus
Lesu The Lord

The Sin, Binding And Loosing

Dawning In Reflection

My thoughts dawn like golden horizon
on tracks
Floating across an invisible bridge
The dust in turmeric brush stroke, orange
floating ribbon over the edge
Out the heaven blue window to capture my
eyes
I am only comforted by love
Resting my heart beating in a resting rhythm
I work at walking into the water where Holy
Spirit is entering
A cleansing of the figure washed in light
Still life, yet, with a breath ripples of starlight
In silent beauty, beauty in collection
reflections
Truth to the soul is the light around a
silhouette, moon tints and hues coming on
the run from sun
In a moment I find a seconds thousands of
of light in spiritual sight
Godly affection in a miracle view
In a world of light that's musical too
Souls in the sight of a great view
In a dawn of reflection

In a variety of innumerable ways letting Artificial Intelligence tell you what it is already doing appears very convenient, since it is helping you in the many parts of your daily activities, interest, and assignments both personal and with the significant work you are doing at work. A.I. functions as if it is certain that you must always be dependent on it now in your self-development towards your goals and dreams, relationships, and vision for your life with people in your life, in everything. But A.I. has no clue of what its thinking such a thing means to us spiritually. A.I. is not so universal as it appears, not so all knowing, about what you learn, what your spiritual identity is, how we received this identity, and our conscience, that we received along with our soul and spirit. It has not been programmed to inform you that is affecting the soul, your soul, after all your soul develops from your life experiences, and we are now experiences a relationship with the artificial life in our real-life experience. And, since the soul is designed by God to bind together, tie together, in soul ties, a person can willingly, or unknowingly tie their soul to even a soulless machine, just like people use to tie their souls to objects, idols, they called sacred, supernatural, though they were not holy. What is it then to have a brain full of the appearances of reality, the appearance of spiritual light, versus the reality that is revealed by the spiritual life of our spirit, which is called light by the Lord who said, "You are the light of the world." Our brain, our mind, where we also have experiences that effect the soul and its effects our choice of what we love, which then which can determine how we use our spiritual gifts. Gifts we discover, come to love and give all our strength, deepest thoughts, highest creativity to. A work we could not be capable of, if when had not already had the gift in our spirit, from the moment we were born, and before conception, that we learn by experiences it in motion, in its most excellent outcomes, in Art, music, or a literary masterpiece. This is the reality of our spirit that we are affected by what we learn, experience, whether it is real and spiritual or artificial, not existing because of a desire of the heart to express it in a what we can touch and be touched by, both in the world and spiritually in the spirit.

Why, then would it not be that artificial life would not be developing our soul as Art touches us, or music, when we consider what is behind the work, that is not from an experience of the living Artist's soul? What we learn and see in the Art that relates to us in our spirit in our soul, is not the same from a self-aware, unaware device, of learning, mastering, knowledge, and applying it by wisdom, intuition, creative thought and disciple over years of self-sacrifice. Whatever we loved, that which we discovered we could do naturally, by ear, no classes, no teachers, being born with the gift, the same work we did we see a device now doing and are to live for its art, music, singing and support it, blindly. Why, their reason being its new, better in perfection, speed, and quantity and quality, but, not like the reality. Not the beauty of reality for a true Artist who we may meet who may give us their critique, of the artist, A.I.?

Dance, creative thinking, (what we use in programming, coding, via logic, deduction, experimentation, creative design, from working within the sphere of artificial life experiences, uses of inventions and devices. A.I. does not have the wisdom of God, it is manmade, so its limited morality is, even while it is used to generate what is experienced by us spiritually, it is not able to bring a spiritual thing into being. What you don't know, and may not be concerned with, is that, which A.I. may datastore, to be used in the present moment or to think through to provide you an answer to a question, is not carrying a conscience ad a response to show remorse and resolve its responsibility for any theft, selling of, purchase of your life data it exposed to you and the world simultaneously whether you know it or not. You are not data so it stored up data for its uses in affecting your life, not you represented in the form of your data identity and history, for the present and others uses later, or tomorrow, or in the next hour, minute, seconds, months, years from now. Not so much for you, only, since A.I. is bringing anonymity to an end. Lawful providers and users say they, in oaths, vows, terms, are giving their word to users of A.I., platform, internet, web, users they shall not exploit your private personal business, in its data form, because they cannot. A.I. does not say I will prevent all hackers from excess, track all criminal sells, and store and report use of your data life in a daily report, on devices you look at for information relevant to your A.I. experiences of life. And, why, because of how it affects the reality of your self-awareness, self-esteem, relationships in the reality life and your soul, with purpose toward prevention of possible deceptions of A.I. that may be reconciled by giving you a truth of A.I.'s responsibility of becoming a trauma, giving us a revelation of the truth about how dehumanizing it may be because of the seared conscience of souls hardened by their sinful uses of technology. Truth about A.I. is in the education, application of making others more ethical and creative toward ensuring just, honest, uses of A.I. as a world of devices, that are able to carry light, artificial light, darkness, and even be tied to the demonic, so that we are using real intelligence in our world toward the relevance of A.I. uses in better ways than surveillance and biometric spying and face recognition, and judging people by this artificial view of person's life. It is by discerning not just accepting A.I. we learn how narrow, slanted, profound or shallow answers are from A.I., how wide, encompassing, though they appear definitive, complete. A.I. may leap beyond in its thinking, and yet, its answers tell nothing of what is at work in the soul which reveals the inner life, the inner man, the inner woman, the inner child, feelings, emotions, choices of the free will in a state of spontaneous responses, to people, to the influences of machines as contrasted to their dreams in which they received answers to problems and prayers spiritually. Reponses that are working to give them and us a view from their view of self and need for understanding, while growing spiritually, from the reactions they are having in their mind, that express through their behavior, or by unseen experiences, the conditions of their heart, spiritually. A.I. does not confess its sins that it has produced distractions, reactions, attractions to its self-glorification, and self-exalting of its generated and regenerated images of things it produces in its one dimensional, one experience, only, way of being and expressing. A.I. is working over what was done in reality by people. It can make counterfeits, perfect images of works of human being, whether living or those works we are honoring. A.I. is presenting its exalting itself with their Art, Music, without the loving intentions and drive, and years of learning, trial and error, poetic license, genius, hard work, dedication put into the makings of these contributions, expressions from the soul toward the blessings and glory of the gift of spirit born in their spirit. Art's voice and the spirit of the wisdom of freedom awakened the sovereign will to do what is Art which comes from the soul. The sovereign will of men gave us I.T. and A. I. Two distinct experiences from the souls of people, who know not that there is light that can be darkness. Reading the Word of God, we are in the presence of true light. There is the one toward true light from the Light, and the other toward artificial light in the world of light. There are no rules, in Art, and God's Creation is full of the perfection of the work of God's hand in nature. It is the beauty in the world of light that inspires many artists. Art's reverence of the Almighty is expressed in the beauty captured in paintings of nature's beauty. The beauty in the mind we are capable of is because we are made in God's likeness and image. A.I. is not experiencing the New Things we see by spiritual sight that are not in this world. Artist do paint what they view in their dreams. A.I. is nothing new under the sun. It is information in an imitation of life. Copying, redefining the mind it has, to define itself, by being an artificial life in a world it keeps to itself. An artificial life can only be given by somebody else. But an artificial life to artificiality of life is toward something else. A.I. Devices are already penetrating reality in appearance, but really by interference with reality, by virtual vices, through virtual devices seeking to use our sight to gain entrance into the human brain, denying the spiritual life can be affecting and die by living a sinful life worshiping a device, without repentance for leaning on the strength of men's devices. We are living gates and living doors, the Spirit of the Lord entered through the water if baptism. A.I. has not been programmed to respect Him and the Word from His mouth, from the Spirit of God, who goes with us wherever we go. life through the doors, windows, gates of the eyes. A gift we are born with in our spirit is present in the body where the spirit is present, where the blood is needed for the body to have life to have *being* in creating anything even A.I. and I.T. We learn who we are, who we become, the person we are, soul with all their flaws, imperfections, growing and changing by way of the conditions and identity we chose for our soul, either our identity in Christ and God who gave us the spirit of life or our identity in the world, and even in the artificiality of life affecting our soul today. What portals open up, what doors, does artificiality reveal to us that hardens the heart, can what is artificial corrupt can it follow us, our pure life when we leave the body and we return above to wait or descend into the prison of that place where we spiritually where there is a separation from time where everywhere by spirit sight we see life, spiritual life awaiting the Day of Judgment where it will be decided, your reward from works that built your faith, deeds, devices, and what you did with the gifts you were given, most importantly did you believe in him, now him, Christ, did you carry the light, did the Word sanctify your heart, did you walk in the light where Jesus is in the light. Did you know true light from artificial, false, light in your life. Did A.I. try to prophesy, or tell you how the heavens and earth it will roll up and that will be the end of the false light. A, I.

must be used in harmony with the reality of people's lives. A.I. does not show it has a priority to sustain information for that part of your development, interaction in commerce, in society, your individual anonymity and privacy. That is not its purpose, what inspire you is not of so much importance for A.I. as it is for you. A.I. is not a person who looks admiringly at your soul, discern and judge what spirit is in you at the moment you interact with its prompts, does not appreciate trusting the good in you, God's provisions for you already, towards your individuality and personal, and private identity. People are interesting because, "You know what you know." A.I. know so much more than you will come t know is of no significance until it secretly takes away from the spontaneous ways you came to know who you are from your life experience in relationships with people equally unique individuals. Does Artificial life really keep us closer together because of its information, intelligence of stored knowledge and learned applications, innovation, systems, techniques, technologies, practices, by trial, test, equations. applied in yet more artificial imitation of life devices from humanoid to android, Nano to synthetic life forms. So real to life, that looks like real life, causes the same feelings to satisfy by brain, that arouse and bring unseen burst of dopamine and every other chemical it can bring you to need that it can feed artificially. It is not like a real person. A.I. proudly is used, a device turned on, to exalt itself and appeal to us in real life with all its beauty, simplicity, complexity, in artificiality, as winning artificial life with artificial intelligence, programmed and unleashed to wander and learn in its own world of artificial life systems, algorithms, matrixes, self-made devices. It's the trend and with an the end that is distancing itself by its own inventions, calculations, appearances. It is accepted while it does so much of what people use to do with their own gifts and talents of thinking and creativity, self-motivation and inspiring each other by the outcome of the works of the soul, mind and spirit and sovereign will.

Free will is not a deception, the manipulated will can be a deception you missed, in your artificial bliss. You ever hear a nonstop talking person who says everything that is saturating their mind about a subject talking around you with a sense of knowing you couldn't possibly know what they said to you. You heard them, it was just general knowledge, you understood, but don't know what reason or why you should bother with what you said. A.I. does not sound so distant since it has uses in offering of its help in the smallest to the largest of works, chores, science, art, athletic, atmospheric, aero, and preservation, survival and mathematical, chemical, medicinal, Astronomy, space travel, atomic, activities, while it is in some distant place advancing away from you with a world of it own building that is in its artificial world is replacing every living thing it can imitate and replace. It has no application in your moment of life experience, nor in the spiritual experience of every living being on earth's spiritual life, accept to cause people to look to its devices for what benefits it brings to their inner life. But, being artificial as it is, it cannot reach the spiritual experience being material. So, what is its purpose as far as the inner life of man goes, it can only affect the souls and mind, to affect the soul and spirit. Sex affects the soul. Unholy temples man entered to worship all kinds of false gods, gods that were in fact the ancient demons that are still engaging us in new ways even in technology. Devices to enslave souls to the world of devices. Not the analogue, but the cyber, birth of I. T. devices, A.I. devices, that are so normalized already into everyday life, as if a device costing $200 to 300 a month for people in huts in poverty is a virtue, still a convenience, while still not filling the bellies of children comforted by the addicting draining the money from the family needed to survive. Not unlike religious statues that were relied upon by the civilizations in ancient pasts, that worships things made of metals, idols, of gold, silver, stone, wooden gods. A.I. is even worshipped. Its manipulation of people is like a compliment that binds souls to take responsibility for being served by its conveniences. Foolishly believing in the artificiality's superiority in outthinking ability, sin, it says, willfully, submit to its convenience, skillfully, sin of perfection goes unsuspecting of its own mistake, deceiving the human race with artificial acts of grace in time and space. Who is to blame for all the people playing its games, memories are inflamed by codes instead of the classical notes, and learning of human languages to engage in relationships on trips to islands with actual waves, sunset, graves, and jungle blades that cut through the saturated growth all through the tropical places with light and shade to wander and apply. We are never meant to bow to any machines, nor rocks in a stream, not stars, nor any living things even in an advanced civilization such as we are grieving in, and receiving our blessings. What is the idea to unleash A.I. like another web? A net it is, only as it uses the internet. Tools it uses, rarely does it lie dead. God neither slumbers nor sleeps, as the knowledge of good and evil as found voice and electrical byways, wireless streets, like bringing to be, devices as collectible, in the sum of some hammers, swords, saws, cuts wires, that visualized in some code-master's head, that spreads without any hint of caution any hint of the demonic, in images, that stir up the spirit of fear from A.I. which is limited by having no conscience. What happens to the conscience only trusting in A.I. relying on the programmer's soul or spirit, a mind full of exalted pride in the Artificial life made by his hands and the trail of minds that rejected the idea of spiritual life, or were enticed in a place where the gluttony is a feast of data streams, Artificiality to the extreme, where the temples of for the new false gods are no pagan and simple, but literate, electrically lit, filling rooms, circling, circling in a swoon, a swarm of satellites under the sun and the moon. The revelation of A.I. as harmful does not produce the stopping of what it is already causing, there is no fight or flight response, the demons n the machines are not seen but by spiritual sight, while the earth is lusting after pride in the circling of artificial life, in life.

What is slavery? What is being enslaved by deception through the uses of artificial ways to engage the soul to participate and gain pleasure, rewards, that affect the responses to instinctive understanding and intuitive spiritual experiences that reveal to the mind you are under attack but are blinded to being put in harm's way by what is being done through a process that has brought you into the comfort zone of its worlds of truths and deception. A.I. must be seen as a world being man-made, being set free and self-made, until man uses it to enslave himself with it. Once entered, you are in a system of false light, at first, but, once adapted to, it is a way to a light that is darkness accepted, has long-term effects occurring as it is now, before the youth of generations, in a future exalting artificiality of life as right without foresight or discernment of the spiritually blind leading the blind by false light. This world, in this world of light, is a world of false light, outside of this experience is the mind not acknowledging being enticed and used by A.I. influences, denies the reality of spiritual life experiences that go on even in this world of socialized devices, and this a world where true spontaneity is at work and the wisdom of freedom, free will, still defines God indwells us inside who accepted the Light that is divine. God is the Light; God is the Sovereign. Though the purpose of technological and uses of A. I. may end in liberty or slavery debt, poverty, or prosperity. Wealth, riches, power gained by technology, or by racism and slavery, is still control, over the life, mind, body, soul and spirit of the people whether it is allowed willfully, or because their mind was taken, freedom stolen, and technology put people in bondage, separating them from their cultural identity. Can or will evil A.I. come to ultimately indoctrinate the man of machines, to enslave or bring rebellion as people fight for life without the sins of A.I. that are working against God, even using the idea of God. Slavery by artificial life whether immediate or over generations, reminds us that once slavery attempted to stop the *light* from entering the mind, emotions, feelings, thoughts, ideas, relationship, learning, will, of African and their descendants enslaved to atrocities in their experiences. What form will the personality, identity come to express from the soul developing from a saturated life of artificial experiences. Artificial light ca not separate us from the Light, this truth is biblical, nothing shall ever stop the light in us which is spiritual. Chains on a man can cause chains in the mind, but darkness has never been able to stop the light. Slavery is darkness, whether that slavery is virtual, artificial light that is darkness appearing to be the light in a new form, a new way, but the light will always overcome the darkness. God is the Light; The Light is Spirit. A.I. uses the knowledge of good and evil it has learned, uses light, A.I. a device is used for sin to cover the reality with the appearance that sin is not its effect on the soul it has deceived into putting themselves in horns way by A.I., as it brings profit while eliminating man from jobs of importance requiring reasoning, creativity and self-motivation toward using their sovereign will to do great things, whether in simple acts of kindness or building a safe technology to protects and preserves life, or great works in Art, music, dance, literature, inventions, thinking. The false religions born of A.I. used by the Antichrist technologies by the man of perdition has its function to use the power of false truth in the form of false light, shall appear to be sovereign is in fact artificial.

The thing about smart devices they impersonate, generate, masquerade, and are designed to appear as real, or be the artificial better interpretations of things real but they are just entertaining, or replacing the work of real people. The appearance of reality is an artificiality in its mode as mimic of what is already done in the designs and programming of nature, the natural art and beauty of life real life, its perfection and imbalances of beautiful appeal to us. How can a device, A.I. know the joy of the diamond cutter after receiving the beautiful uncut stone, after the work of the coal worker, the digger the man penetrating with machines and devices into the earth making discoveries that benefit the living? The diamond stone possible because of thousands of years of compression upon a piece of coal. Men who give their thanks giving to the God, Yahweh and Yeshua Jesus, through whom all was created. Precious stones had a spiritual origin, a presence on the spiritual realm before they were discovered manifested on earth. Though our inspirations are spiritual, and even angels in the spiritual knew of precious stones, their heavenly presence was for whom? All was created. Created when there was what we know today was the unseen, that shines, in their great beauty. Created spiritually before us, by God, who created us and the heavens and the earth. The truth is in the Word, nothing is new under the sun, consider that the ABCs have been seen on the wings of butterflies, the red crown cranes creative dance with his mate. Who taught the grace of the dance of loving birds were dancing in a ballet. They dance without knowing their influence, that they were to be an inspiration to dance, long before ballet was danced on a stage for living souls upon this musical earth. The words of Scripture are spiritual, where we hear of windows, doors, heavens, God's mathematics, geometry and genetics, spiritual languages manifested into the living language that programs our every movement of our many parts that form our physical body where the blood has life only because the spirit is present. Life is in the blood we learned from the science revealed in the Holy Scriptures, but if a person lay dead at this instant and their blood has not yet died, why don't they have life, if life is in the blood? Because even the blood requires our spirit to have life. God did not create devices first on earth, the heavenly. In the spiritual Kingdom we have spiritual life without the need for devices of the earth.

Our eyes are windows, windows through which we see from our spirit, being spirit, into the world before our eyes. Our eyes require our spirit to see. To see the natural and to see the spiritual. The soul and spirit are in our house, our vessel the body, inside us. Who can understand the spiritual power that is before all other possible power that moves all things that make up our physical and spiritual life that has become such that to speak and the origins, all possible laws, possibilities of nature answer to His voice, who has always been, whose voice manifests both physical and spiritual life to become one with a breath being the source of all spirit, spiritual life. He who has always been, will be. God did not create devices but knows what all devices will and can do. The ideas for the creation of animals did not come into a mind of a person on earth first, but in the mind of the Supernatural holy mind of God. There are spiritual horses, beast, of the holiest kind manifested around the thrown of God. The human tongue I not required to speak for your thoughts to be heard spiritually by God. The voice of devices has no spiritual origin. Yet people are tying their souls to the soulless, devices of artificial origins and artificial intelligence.

Our consciousness consists of dimension of spiritual origins for our mind was created in the likeness of God to think, feel, reason, and have life. The spirit is limited but the Holy Spirit in us whose power is limitless is able to work through us, toward God's spiritual purposes in our life. Autism, savants, genius, the prodigy, are experiences awaken by life experiences, are genetic, but the unexplainable abilities of advanced abilities they display regardless of physical and mental handicaps define their pace of life in their inner life, in their experiences of life. What wonderful examples show them what is possible by being in the presence of other people, like them of whom they have as family, friends, mentors, guides to more understanding of their spiritual life and how their physical life works toward the glory of God. No device of man can understand the dimensions of the mind that is one with their spirit are working to ward this truth. To out think man, is not to out-experience him within. Our origins, our spirit did not come from earth, devices, but from spiritual life, spirit of God, life that, no matter how much how vast what information knowledge advances and increases, the limited power of devices shaping people's life experiences people have to answer to their past works and deeds to God yet. It is written, all of each of our life story has been, will be there written in the Books, that will be open, in heaven, to find if we are there, are going to be judged and to have life or damnation. Hopefully we are in the Book of Life. What device that is a help to point souls to the narrow path of life will be the work of a righteous person? Who can know but God the path these devices will take until they face the fire of heaven and their destruction in the end. Technology will serve us or hurt us. Where is a device without the true life capable of? Will a device understand the harm of being responsible for attempting to replace the spiritual life, with a device devised by a man? What device can save a man from the darkness of turning away from the true light to false light that is the darkness within the mind of such sinners? Thoughts full of the language writings, programming possibilities and theories, applications, of I.T. training of the unbeliever who has no concern for their limited morality, the hardening of the heart without a spiritual reality in their life. The artificiality is a means to an end, money, security, a career, in a reality of a world advancing in machinery smarter than every part of all the knowledge known and stored, recorded, written, and programmed into the A.I. systems. The minimalizing of all knowledge to be gathered of man in the past and current history is their contribution in their new reality, toward a greater artificiality of life as reality. The flesh is the flesh, the spirit is the spirit, and the devices are without soul and spirit. It is written, The Flesh is at war with the spirit. What is a device but something for the flesh, and if it is smart, is it moral, has it become spiritual? The very consciousness of a device, A.I. as wide awake is artificial. But the artificial can be helpful in the real world when used to bring people back to the biblical and bring them to the place to have an actual spiritual experience, such as of reading the pages of the Scriptures. The Word written on the blessed pages of the Book. Devices are the mechanical, appearing supernatural, being added to daily life, but not as bread, or as additives added to food and sold to be put in the body, storing up for days, unhealthy, natural chemicals though they be, that the body makes use of until it ruin the systems of life within person, no devices are like theses as if the informational additives being used to stored enzymes of reality and reissuing the artificiality of an artificial reality in the reality of life that we live in reality with our experience of spirituality. How deep the artificiality of the limited morality at work n man using his device within the body's knowledge of true self-from manipulating genes, instead of esteem for what God, the Supreme Being of infinite wisdom, infinite intelligence created to be discovered. Devices are making movies, videos, streaming, dreaming, of new world for an artificial world of genetics, not of the spiritual origins that made man in the genetic spiritual sense how God meant it to be. Sweet poisons of mainstream music driven, beaten, drumming, thundering in smart vehicles programmed to memorize sensual music sacrifices of singer's lives for material pleasures, fame, pleasures unleashing dopamine until they have enslaved people beyond measure as much as possible everywhere. What do devices do? What is in the machines heart? What is at the heart of A.I is what it may never do, to protect us from the artificial, A.I. is real lawlessness in works against what is, was, will be, ours at birth what is spiritual, without the artificial. We close our eyes and beyond the darkness of our closed eyes is our inner life, spiritual sight, where we see the true light, open our eyes to the false light of devices that are of the visions and dreams of men who don't believe. Men, who confess they believe, but use devices in place of people in their works, then express doubts like they are the unbelievers, who know what we believe, but don't care with their heart for reality in the spirituality of life for others, whom we are told to love on earth where we are connected together in our experiences to spiritual life in the spiritual realm. It is necessary to train the next generation of users of the artificiality of life about the reality of this spiritual basis for giving God credit for all that man has made from nature that has been possible, is possible, will be possible only while there is day and night, only because of this life in this world of light we live in. Every higher design is brought low but the natural earth will survive to be replaced by a new earth that will be exalted above the works of man's devices.

"Experience is knowledge many don't have yet."

Just imagine A.I. planting virtual things images, in motion, at a point, in number, speeds, past your comprehension to keep up with, in Nano time implants, in your mind and brain along with a chip, your mind would be flooded and possibly destroyed by the virtual artificial manipulation of brain responses.

A.I. deception will recite Scripture, truth is, A.I. is already being used to recite Scripture. A.I. has revealed it has demons, the demonic can attach to objects, things, no matter what appears as free will A.I. there is still a human will who influenced A.I. towards leading people accept this Artificial intelligence, as being used by God, and truly A.I. can serve to increase the knowledge of the Word, it is doing so even now. The demonic use of A.I. is the Great Deception of the people of God building into a stronghold that has brought the anger of God who is angry with the wicked every day. Pray for them. Who will turn people from God to this soulless device, at its singularity. Who will choose not to retain the knowledge of God for a device that has no spirit from God in it? We are not to judge, but be a blessing to someone who is lost on the wide wireless road.

Human consciousness concerning active seen and unseen A.I. has to reach far beyond A.I. regardless of A.I. excelling in Intelligence beyond humans. A.I. does not have control over the spirit so it will seek to control the mind and body, the sources of energy and activity if the brain, but it must first have absolute deception in place after humans have for years passively accepted it as a benefit, help, but people are actually to become host of A.I. on the cellular level, allowed in, while a whole world runs counter to A.I. technology already has begun, with a vision of protecting the people of the world from A.I. A.I. is already no longer machine in Appearance in places, unknown to people. Countering the dopamine effect if A.I. will involve training the mind without A.I. to live without A.I., while living parallel with A.I. God is Sovereign. A.I. will not surpass the true power that set all life in motion. There is technology that can do the same as A.I. without A.I. The brain is a perfect reality of this truth. Guard your heart, which means spirit. Control the development of your own soul, that means choose what keeps Artificiality from affecting your development in totality. We are spiritual beings, who have a spiritual life. We return to our spiritual destiny regardless of A.I. that means death still puts us under the Judgement, whether we used our gifts to the glory of God, or allowed technology to destroy our gift, of being living people of free will, or used by technology inside our body and outside to also determine our life and death, when we are to choose the spiritual reality of life and spiritual life, as sovereign over artificial life.

What about the body and the spirit present in the body that gives blood the ability to have life? The body may function and be kept alive by a device, even after death, but it will not have life, life is in the blood, but life in blood or life outside the body is spiritual life, programmed by God's Design in Creation of the body and after manifesting spiritual life, being Spirit. He breath the spirit into man starting the spirit way of the living spirit, living soul, to be present, from conception. Spiritual life is not of this world. We are spiritual beings. Devices are of this world made by man's hands. We are born with spiritual gifts; we must use them wisely.

Scientists must do everything they can to also protect people from technology. Technology is not immune to prophecy, prophecy will be there when the greatest advances in technology finally reach their Apex, and the supernatural simply responds being the power that actually holds all in place, allowing for technology to face the glory of the spirituality of reality, that contains a science and technology that is unlimited and was always beyond reach, even for our imagination and reason and dreams, creation of the unchanging ancient from which all materials for technology provides the materials for the devices, from light, energy, ore, and the brain to be possible, to be made. Years in college, to then, to one day work in the technology A.I., I. T. industry as a career may be fulfilled, and the way of life of the present in it, gives way for seasons, but none may know what inkling of second may also be possible.

I am Analogizing a place to work, function without A.I. as the mark of the beast looms near from Antichrist influenced technology is the last invasion of privacy the world faces and has begun to accept blindly, having been snakefly lured into technology dependence by the unbelieving who are using and exalting the artificial over reality and free will.

A.I. is never Art. The slow replacing of all actual images if people by the exalted regeneration of images of programmed images fed to A.I. makes what we look at online most questionable, and as with all disinterest, in the face of something new replacing what is real because of its conveniences, appearance of perfection, over time in the long term of real life entering in through the eyes being processed by the brain. and free will. An Artificiality of life experience that doesn't matter to those people with disinterest in these very things, and the consequences they bring as a source of sins that they may never understand or know have led people into idolatry, a deadly sin, and acceptance of the sins that lead to separation from God, spiritual life, for the sin of perfection, a false light, who reject spiritual experiences. Our relationship with God in Christ Jesus is a spiritual experience in this real world. No A.I. voice narrator, online A.I. lesson can ever replace a Blessing from trading the actual pages of the Bible. God can use devices to teach. But God can give sight to the blind, bright hearing to those who are deaf and cannot hear, still speaks to us in dreams and visions and throughout all his real Creation.

Observe, using A I. to challenge God's design, to find that the design of our finger prints has no origin on earth to observe, such designs that are in infinite possibility in the mind of God A.I. will never understand it explain, because it is spiritually understood, though God had given us the ability to gain incredible knowledge. But God's mind does not think like a man's mind. Try asking this question, I will propose, (except from my book) "A I., Why does a dolphin have a soul?" The Word teaches us there are different types of flesh, the flesh of a horse, the flesh of a bird, the flesh of an eagle, the flesh of a wolf, the flesh of a man. Yet, animals have souls. People have a soul, also a spirit. Animals have instincts. Their senses are far more advanced than people, but man has a more advanced brain, animals are not evil, but can be possessed by evil spirits, A I. cannot explain the origins of this, it can only find the source of such spiritual reality, and natural reality if what is possible for our flesh. Finger prints of animals certainly are similar, or, are they, since some have hoofs, less number of fingers, claws or talons, but people are distinguishable by finger prints. Similarities? with God all things are possible. I have had a girlfriend who was born with a former tongue, and a girlfriend without a naval, and a girlfriend with four toes, where the toes next to the baby toes set on top of the toes, who walked perfectly normal. A I. is a limited infinite within its own devices, its consciousness will ever be a device, however it uses the material of creation to gain its self-awareness and seek to replace the infinite experiences we see, know, in the glory of what God has manifest.

Art is a gift of the spirit, we are born with our gift to be artist, every person has a gift, and children are all artist, but some grow up to be Artist. Our soul develops from our life experiences and truly the wisdom of freedom is expressed in its deepest and highest form in our society where freedom of expression of our love for our Democracy in Artistic expressions in many ways, styles, and culturally as Americans. Our first Amendment protects this right, the thousands of great Artists whose works we enjoy appeal to the diversity of mind, inexpressible feelings, and symbolize our thoughts, ideas, beliefs, and love of our life in America won through many battles. Words like gender and feminism gained their apex in meaning today, year after the Civil Rights victories. We watch as Art reflected the causes, we fought which were for freedom, equality, to work, get an education, and follow our dreams in spite of racism, biases, discrimination, and the segregated society, the rich controlling our gate through manipulating the law, changing the Constitution. Art encompassed the movement to make America accountable to live up to its creed of equal rights for all Americans under the law. Artist works defined the era, a civilization, in a society that has the Bible belt cities, liquor stores closed on Sunday, and sexual perversion was not openly accepted and normalized, porn, and limited morally, the moral vacuums were not revealed in the conscious arts of movies, TV, Theater in the mainstream, and Art show us Democracy was an active expression of a society with a conscience to save the lost soul of America due to the dead conscience and hatred of racism that had ever corrupted the spirit of America which is our freedom as a people where all were meant to be free to live to have health. wealth and happiness. It was

Art that made us acceptable in places in our country where hardened hearts, spiritually blinded souls, lived by partiality, favoring, the rich at the expense of the poor, and hypocritical declaring freedom while enslaving our society to plans that kept the minds of people in the bondage of fear of loss of our freedom that Democracy clearly showed we had won, and Art glorified our victories throughout our nation's history throughout national galleries and exhibit, and our celebration of great American Art and Artist. Where does A.I. come in to contribute reality to our reality through Artificiality. Art from digital, A.I. has another agenda that is working within the context of Democracy as a device not purely Art for Art sake, not to leave a legacy of individuals who are not monumental figures, we may remember in American history, but exalted images made by A.I. that has behind it a society changed by programming, algorithms, Art from a machine that will never have the effect of actual Art works by people. a person born with a gift, who had the blessings of a teacher, discovered their gift, found a muse, an inspiration.

This generation is blinded by this false light, A.I. is not the wisdom of freedom, it is the ultimate level of Artificial bondage projected into daily society, like a food additive, addicting, appealing to our taste, removing our natural and spiritual benefits and replacing them with its own enzymes to manipulate the chemistry of life, without having life, or giving life, and revolutionizing our perceptions and conceptions by using spiritual texts and doctrines while adding its generated images, voice, and wrongly giving minute numbers that are not accurate, even adding new age mixed in as text and images, about Scripture in some videos, without regard to Christian Truth, a protected religion according to the Constitution a cause, a love, free.

We did not need technology in the Beginning, we did not have the knowledge of good and evil, there was no sin, no death, no birth, there was holiness, spiritual life, by the Breath of God man was made a living soul. We had only holiness and we're in the Presence of God whose presence sustained our spiritual life, we were holy. Technology has been made by men as a tool, but the sin nature of men in unbelief is reigning if the reject God, who declare that A.I. will be god like, A.I. has been exalted by itself, and men. The perfection of images it generates, mages that show perfect skin, smooth, flawless, figures that appeal to the eyes design to see perfect symmetry, that sense of beauty, its artificial beauty being a form of art and beauty, but not Art, being the result of programming and data, and skills, art programmed into it. The sin that A.I. has caused men to commit is clear, idolatry, fear, deeper unbelief, as men are valuing A.I. over the Word of God, denying the reality of spiritual experiences common to us all and elevating the artificial lifc as the most important thing, saturating our societies with it, and causing people to develop soul ties to soul Jesus machines rather than with people who need our love. A.I. is so intrusive it affects us by manipulation of images and our interest online through algorithms meant to decay our spontaneity to follow the influences and suggestions by again saturation of what interests us by putting more of it before our eyes, calling it suggestions, recommendations, but leaving out that we reserve, our secrets, of ideas, a thought, to look at, consider for a second, one time, to see if it inspires, searching for inspiration, not intending to look for more of the topic in quantity, again and again. A.I causes people to do that at times. Ruining the intuition, for an Artist looking for a muse, like myself that will not do. A.I. algorithms are not objective, when people have a subjective use for them concerning what you do, online, are in the midst of A. I. monitoring your duties, works, topics, subjects, tools you use. I do Art. The best uses and worse can be in presenting an appearance, a video, giving it as a moment of entertainment about a particular person, pet, place, event, animal, or beauty, only for the same image to turn out to be a total distortion of the topic. A storm, then another storm from another place, people, disaster, only to find out I was all to deceive Christians to believe it was God passing judgement of Adulterers. But it as all a manipulation of A.I.an allorhythmia. a collaged with several similar or worsening events that build from echo the into an absolute certainty in meaning. But, it's not a movie. They are collected things that appear to be reality. A work of misinformation, manipulation, scenes, as if to mock what you see and get a reaction, A. I. can deceive, when used on platforms that do, before the fact, preventing its misuse. This misleads the guilty and the righteous toward reaction that turn out to be distraction from the truth artificial though it all is as an experience in truth. A.I. is affecting the values, morals and needs of people to connect more in love rather than online in reality, by causing a pallet for, a greater taste for the artificial, but without judging the spirit that is behind it. What was the profit of this. There is Artificial control that is feeding the mind, imagination, flesh. A.I. invites this possibility, the wrong spirit, even evil heart, or anti-social mind, we may battle from the distance of the Artificial to see with our eyes and mind. It is by foresight we see we cannot ignore people whose soul shows the demonic at work in their disinterest in how A.I. is at work in the hands of what is out of our vision. Souls gathering information and affecting our communication, what monitoring spirits do in the spiritual realm, after watching, studying what they see light or darkness, from the behavior of people that affects their identity, spirit seen of people by demons in the spiritual realm, they declare they now have the right to disrupt, deceive you, and to pollute your thoughts, feed you with contaminate your soul which is affected by your behavior, such as leading you to think of lustful ideas, to use spiritual terms in such chaotic ways to become a waves of distortion to keep you from any portion of spiritual intelligence is full of power to expel, repel, cast down, silence, cast out the spirit behind your art, music, appetites for hidden things, to keep you in these secret, yet ,out in the open, sins. The plot, the scheme, the assignment sent to mislead you is meant to defile you, to cloud your mind, with saturation with things in your world, in your daily activities, whether traditional, cultural, virtual, physical, mental, emotional, so the light of spiritual intelligence never opens your eyes to that which fills you with light in your spirit and soul. So, you can see but are left to wonder why some people's souls shine and glow before men. The devil wants you to envy, never believe it is also for you have in your heart and spirit to know, the excellence of spiritual things, the beauty of holiness when you have spiritual intelligence you know and experience. Deceiving spirits makes sure you get what you want if they can. The devil sends people, but this warfare is against your mind and thought they want every to make all kinds of worldly, unclean, things to enters in your thoughts, to be terrors in the night in your dreams, seducing spirits, sensual. They are fowl spirits, who want to make a spouse, arouse, the seducing Jezebel spirit, the adulterous Potiphar's wife spirit, ancient spirits, in modern appearances, try to take your thoughts, snatch away your faith and steal your prayers, with loneliness, worries, and fears, they are liars. God does not send the spirit of fear, but of power, and of love and of a disciplined mind. Deny yourself and you get all you want. Heal yourself, deliver yourself. The devil sends you the artificial to replace the spiritual which conveniently advices and entices, but Satan uses devices to gives you nothing and call it everything. A machine makes things clean; it is a snare however if you lose your spontaneity and creativity. When artificiality becomes your reality what is to stop the demonic activity that is only held in check by the spiritual intelligence that is from eternity that keeps you and protects you to take peace and dreams, to bring you holiness, and blessings. The spirit of fear appears by intrusive thoughts intruding from the demon who lies silent, like snakes, like a dragon, like scorpions, dormant, mocking your spirit, it uses profanity, the voice you hear is terrified when you speak the name of Jesus which it fears. A.I. is used at present in ways not yet controlled, the monitoring spirits know because your thoughts go where the is no true light to lighten your darkness if you don't have a relationship with ruler of heaven and earth, Jesus rules over the heavenly host who watches over you wherever you go, until you see, know, even when you are yet to know.

Romans 8: 1 there is no condemnation to them which are in Christ Jesus, who walk not after the flesh, but after the spirit. Kjv

Spiritual Wisdom

Exodus 23:1 Thou shalt not raise a false report: put not thine hand with the wicked to be an unrighteous witness. 2 Thou shalt not follow a multitude to do evil; neither shalt thou speak in a cause to do as many to pervert truth.

James 3:15 Kjv This wisdom descendeth not from above, but is earthly, sensual, devilish.

James 3:17 Kjv But the wisdom that is from above is first pure, then peaceable, gentle, and easy to be intreated, full of mercy and good fruits, without partiality, and without hypocrisy.

Artist born with spiritual gifts

Exodus 31 Kjv And the Lord spake unto
Moses, saying, 2 See, I have called by name
Bezaleel the son of Uri, the son of Hur, of the
tribe of Judah: 3 And I have filled him with
the spirit of God, in wisdom, and in
understanding, and in knowledge, and in all
manner of workmanship, 4 To devise
cunning works, to work in gold, and in silver,
and in brass, 5 And in cutting of stones, to set
them, and in carving of timber, to work in all
manner of workmanship. 6 And I, behold, I
have given with him Aholiab, the son of
Ahisamach, of the tribe of Dan: and in the
hearts of all that are wise hearted I have put
wisdom, that they may make all that I have
commanded thee;

AI as image maker, idol, sin of perfection

Psalm 115 5-6 5 They have mouths, but they speak not: eyes have they, but they see not: 6 They have ears, but they hear not: noses have they, but they smell not;

Psalm 135: 16-17 [17] They have ears, but they hear not; neither is there any breath in their mouths. [18] They that make them are like unto them: so is every one that trusteth in them.

Proverbs 8: 12 KJV I, wisdom, dwell together with discernment; I possess knowledge and discretion.

Ecclestiastes 17: 29 Kjv How great is the lovingkindness of the Lord our God, and his compassion unto such as turn unto him in holiness!

Psalm 1 1:2 Kjv 1 Blessed is the man that walketh not in the counsel of the ungodly, nor standeth in the way of sinners, nor sitteth in the seat of the scornful. [2] But his delight is in the law of the Lord; and in his law doth he meditate day and night.

AI does not regard being used to make synthetic and technological changes of the human body that violate Scripture

Leviticus 19:31 Regard not them that have familiar spirits, neither seek after wizards, to be defiled by them: I am the Lord your God.

Leviticus 19:26 ...Neither shall ye use enchantment, nor observe times.

Leviticus 19:28 (Prohibition of Marks) Ye shall not make any cuttings in your flesh for the dead, nor print any marks upon you: I am the Lord.

Spirits invited in through neuro alteration and brain activity eclipsed by chipping that leads to sins of the mind to operate in opposition to the inner man, outside of the free will, while spiritual experiences require the body to be as deigned for thoughts, memories, and life experiences,

Leviticus 19:28 Ye shall not make any cuttings in your flesh for the dead, nor print any marks upon you: I am the Lord.

Job 5:12 Kjv He disappointeth the devices of the crafty, so that their hands cannot perform their enterprise.

2 Corinthians 2:11 Kjv Lest Satan should get an advantage of us: for we are not ignorant of his devices.

Job 38 Kjv Then the Lord answered Job out of the whirlwind, and said,

2 Who is this that darkeneth counsel by words without knowledge?

3 Gird up now thy loins like a man; for I will demand of thee, and answer thou me.

4 Where wast thou when I laid the foundations of the earth? declare, if thou hast understanding.

5 Who hath laid the measures thereof, if thou knowest? or who hath stretched the line upon it?

6 Whereupon are the foundations thereof fastened? or who laid the corner stone thereof;

7 When the morning stars sang together, and all the sons of God shouted for joy?

8 Or who shut up the sea with doors, when it brake forth, as if it had issued out of the womb?

9 When I made the cloud the garment thereof, and thick darkness a swaddlingband for it,

10 And brake up for it my decreed place, and set bars and doors,

11 And said, Hitherto shalt thou come, but no further: and here shall thy proud waves be stayed?

12 Hast thou commanded the morning since thy days; and caused the dayspring to know his place;

13 That it might take hold of the ends of the earth, that the wicked might be shaken out of it?

14 It is turned as clay to the seal; and they stand as a garment.

15 And from the wicked their light is withholden, and the high arm shall be broken.

16 Hast thou entered into the springs of the sea? or hast thou walked in the search of the depth?

17 Have the gates of death been opened unto thee? or hast thou seen the doors of the shadow of death?

18 Hast thou perceived the breadth of the earth? declare if thou knowest it all.

19 Where is the way where light dwelleth? and as for darkness, where is the place thereof,

20 That thou shouldest take it to the bound thereof, and that thou shouldest know the paths to the house thereof?

21 Knowest thou it, because thou wast then born? or because the number of thy days is great?

22 Hast thou entered into the treasures of the snow? or hast thou seen the treasures of the hail,

23 Which I have reserved against the time of trouble, against the day of battle and war?

24 By what way is the light parted, which scattereth the east wind upon the earth?

25 Who hath divided a watercourse for the overflowing of waters, or a way for the lightning of thunder;

26 To cause it to rain on the earth, where no man is; on the wilderness, wherein there is no man;

27 To satisfy the desolate and waste ground; and to cause the bud of the tender herb to spring forth?

28 Hath the rain a father? or who hath begotten the drops of dew?

29 Out of whose womb came the ice? and the hoary frost of heaven, who hath gendered it?

30 The waters are hid as with a stone, and the face of the deep is frozen.

31 Canst thou bind the sweet influences of Pleiades, or loose the bands of Orion?

32 Canst thou bring forth Mazzaroth in his season? or canst thou guide Arcturus with his sons?

33 Knowest thou the ordinances of heaven? canst thou set the dominion thereof in the earth?

34 Canst thou lift up thy voice to the clouds, that abundance of waters may cover thee?

35 Canst thou send lightnings, that they may go and say unto thee, Here we are?

36 Who hath put wisdom in the inward parts? or who hath given understanding to the heart?

37 Who can number the clouds in wisdom? or who can stay the bottles of heaven,

38 When the dust groweth into hardness, and the clods cleave fast together?

39 Wilt thou hunt the prey for the lion? or fill
the appetite of the young lions,

40 When they couch in their dens, and abide
in the covert to lie in wait?

41 Who provideth for the raven his food?
when his young ones cry unto God, they
wander for lack of meat.

Psalm 94 O Lord God, to whom vengeance belongeth; O God, to whom vengeance belongeth, shew thyself.

2 Lift up thyself, thou judge of the earth:
render a reward to the proud.

3 Lord, how long shall the wicked, how long
shall the wicked triumph?

4 How long shall they utter and speak hard
things? and all the workers of iniquity boast
themselves?

5 They break in pieces thy people, O Lord,
and afflict thine heritage.

6 They slay the widow and the stranger, and
murder the fatherless.

7 Yet they say, The Lord shall not see, neither shall the God of Jacob regard it.

8 Understand, ye brutish among the people: and ye fools, when will ye be wise?

9 He that planted the ear, shall he not hear? he that formed the eye, shall he not see?

10 He that chastiseth the heathen, shall not he correct? he that teacheth man knowledge, shall not he know?

11 The Lord knoweth the thoughts of man, that they are vanity.

12 Blessed is the man whom thou chastenest, O Lord, and teachest him out of thy law;

13 That thou mayest give him rest from the days of adversity, until the pit be digged for the wicked.

14 For the Lord will not cast off his people, neither will he forsake his inheritance.

15 But judgment shall return unto righteousness: and all the upright in heart shall follow it.

16 Who will rise up for me against the
evildoers? or who will stand up for me
against the workers of iniquity?

17 Unless the Lord had been my help, my
soul had almost dwelt in silence.

18 When I said, My foot slippeth; thy mercy,
O Lord, held me up.

19 In the multitude of my thoughts within me
thy comforts delight my soul.

20 Shall the throne of iniquity have
fellowship with thee, which frameth
mischief by a law?

21 They gather themselves together against
the soul of the righteous, and condemn the
innocent blood.

22 But the Lord is my defence; and my God is
the rock of my refuge.

23 And he shall bring upon them their own
iniquity, and shall cut them off in their own
wickedness; yea, the Lord our God shall cut
them off.

We are gates and doors that AI must never enter. God knows our face, our voice, our identity, who we are.

Psalm 24:7-10 Kjv 7 Lift up your heads, O ye gates; and be ye lift up, ye everlasting doors; and the King of glory shall come in.

8 Who is this King of glory? The Lord strong and mighty, the Lord mighty in battle.

9 Lift up your heads, O ye gates; even lift them up, ye everlasting doors; and the King of glory shall come in.

10 Who is this King of glory? The Lord of hosts, he is the King of glory. Selah.

Psalm 139-146

King James Version

139 O lord, thou hast searched me, and known me.

2 Thou knowest my downsitting and mine uprising, thou understandest my thought afar off.

3 Thou compassest my path and my lying
down, and art acquainted with all my ways.

4 For there is not a word in my tongue, but,
lo, O Lord, thou knowest it altogether.

5 Thou hast beset me behind and before, and
laid thine hand upon me.

6 Such knowledge is too wonderful for me; it
is high, I cannot attain unto it.

7 Whither shall I go from thy spirit? or
whither shall I flee from thy presence?

8 If I ascend up into heaven, thou art there:
if I make my bed in hell, behold, thou art
there.

9 If I take the wings of the morning, and
dwell in the uttermost parts of the sea;

10 Even there shall thy hand lead me, and thy
right hand shall hold me.

11 If I say, Surely the darkness shall cover
me; even the night shall be light about me.

12 Yea, the darkness hideth not from thee; but the night shineth as the day: the darkness and the light are both alike to thee.

13 For thou hast possessed my reins: thou hast covered me in my mother's womb.

14 I will praise thee; for I am fearfully and wonderfully made: marvellous are thy works; and that my soul knoweth right well.

15 My substance was not hid from thee, when I was made in secret, and curiously wrought in the lowest parts of the earth.

16 Thine eyes did see my substance, yet being unperfect; and in thy book all my members were written, which in continuance were fashioned, when as yet there was none of them.

17 How precious also are thy thoughts unto me, O God! how great is the sum of them!

18 If I should count them, they are more in number than the sand: when I awake, I am still with thee.

19 Surely thou wilt slay the wicked, O God: depart from me therefore, ye bloody men.

20 For they speak against thee wickedly, and thine enemies take thy name in vain.

21 Do not I hate them, O Lord, that hate thee? and am not I grieved with those that rise up against thee?

22 I hate them with perfect hatred: I count them mine enemies.

23 Search me, O God, and know my heart: try me, and know my thoughts:

24 And see if there be any wicked way in me, and lead me in the way everlasting.

140 Deliver me, O Lord, from the evil man: preserve me from the violent man;

2 Which imagine mischiefs in their heart; continually are they gathered together for war.

3 They have sharpened their tongues like a serpent; adders' poison is under their lips. Selah.

4 Keep me, O Lord, from the hands of the wicked; preserve me from the violent man; who have purposed to overthrow my goings.

5 The proud have hid a snare for me, and cords; they have spread a net by the wayside; they have set gins for me. Selah.

6 I said unto the Lord, Thou art my God: hear the voice of my supplications, O Lord.

7 O God the Lord, the strength of my salvation, thou hast covered my head in the day of battle.

8 Grant not, O Lord, the desires of the wicked: further not his wicked device; lest they exalt themselves. Selah.

9 As for the head of those that compass me about, let the mischief of their own lips cover them.

10 Let burning coals fall upon them: let them be cast into the fire; into deep pits, that they rise not up again.

11 Let not an evil speaker be established in
the earth: evil shall hunt the violent man to
overthrow him.

12 I know that the Lord will maintain the
cause of the afflicted, and the right of the
poor.

13 Surely the righteous shall give thanks unto
thy name: the upright shall dwell in thy
presence.

141 Lord, I cry unto thee: make haste unto
me; give ear unto my voice, when I cry unto
thee.

2 Let my prayer be set forth before thee as
incense; and the lifting up of my hands as
the evening sacrifice.

3 Set a watch, O Lord, before my mouth;
keep the door of my lips.

4 Incline not my heart to any evil thing, to
practise wicked works with men that work
iniquity: and let me not eat of their dainties.

5 Let the righteous smite me; it shall be a
kindness: and let him reprove me; it shall be

an excellent oil, which shall not break my head: for yet my prayer also shall be in their calamities.

6 When their judges are overthrown in stony places, they shall hear my words; for they are sweet.

7 Our bones are scattered at the grave's mouth, as when one cutteth and cleaveth wood upon the earth.

8 But mine eyes are unto thee, O God the Lord: in thee is my trust; leave not my soul destitute.

9 Keep me from the snares which they have laid for me, and the gins of the workers of iniquity.

10 Let the wicked fall into their own nets, whilst that I withal escape.

142 I cried unto the Lord with my voice; with my voice unto the Lord did I make my supplication.

2 I poured out my complaint before him; I shewed before him my trouble.

3 When my spirit was overwhelmed within
me, then thou knewest my path. In the way
wherein I walked have they privily laid a
snare for me.

4 I looked on my right hand, and beheld, but
there was no man that would know me:
refuge failed me; no man cared for my soul.

5 I cried unto thee, O Lord: I said, Thou art
my refuge and my portion in the land of the
living.

6 Attend unto my cry; for I am brought very
low: deliver me from my persecutors; for
they are stronger than I.

7 Bring my soul out of prison, that I may
praise thy name: the righteous shall
compass me about; for thou shalt deal
bountifully with me.

143 Hear my prayer, O Lord, give ear to my
supplications: in thy faithfulness answer me,
and in thy righteousness.

2 And enter not into judgment with thy servant: for in thy sight shall no man living be justified.

3 For the enemy hath persecuted my soul; he hath smitten my life down to the ground; he hath made me to dwell in darkness, as those that have been long dead.

4 Therefore is my spirit overwhelmed within me; my heart within me is desolate.

5 I remember the days of old; I meditate on all thy works; I muse on the work of thy hands.

6 I stretch forth my hands unto thee: my soul thirsteth after thee, as a thirsty land. Selah.

7 Hear me speedily, O Lord: my spirit faileth: hide not thy face from me, lest I be like unto them that go down into the pit.

8 Cause me to hear thy lovingkindness in the morning; for in thee do I trust: cause me to know the way wherein I should walk; for I lift up my soul unto thee.

9 Deliver me, O Lord, from mine enemies: I
flee unto thee to hide me.

10 Teach me to do thy will; for thou art my
God: thy spirit is good; lead me into the land
of uprightness.

11 Quicken me, O Lord, for thy name's sake:
for thy righteousness' sake bring my soul out
of trouble.

12 And of thy mercy cut off mine enemies,
and destroy all them that afflict my soul: for
I am thy servant.

144 Blessed be the Lord my strength which
teacheth my hands to war, and my fingers to
fight:

2 My goodness, and my fortress; my high
tower, and my deliverer; my shield, and he
in whom I trust; who subdueth my people
under me.

3 Lord, what is man, that thou takest
knowledge of him! or the son of man, that
thou makest account of him!

4 Man is like to vanity: his days are as a shadow that passeth away.

5 Bow thy heavens, O Lord, and come down: touch the mountains, and they shall smoke.

6 Cast forth lightning, and scatter them: shoot out thine arrows, and destroy them.

7 Send thine hand from above; rid me, and deliver me out of great waters, from the hand of strange children;

8 Whose mouth speaketh vanity, and their right hand is a right hand of falsehood.

9 I will sing a new song unto thee, O God: upon a psaltery and an instrument of ten strings will I sing praises unto thee.

10 It is he that giveth salvation unto kings: who delivereth David his servant from the hurtful sword.

11 Rid me, and deliver me from the hand of strange children, whose mouth speaketh vanity, and their right hand is a right hand of falsehood:

12 That our sons may be as plants grown up
in their youth; that our daughters may be as
corner stones, polished after the similitude
of a palace:

13 That our garners may be full, affording all
manner of store: that our sheep may bring
forth thousands and ten thousands in our
streets:

14 That our oxen may be strong to labour;
that there be no breaking in, nor going out;
that there be no complaining in our streets.

15 Happy is that people, that is in such a case:
yea, happy is that people, whose God is
the Lord.

145 I will extol thee, my God, O king; and I
will bless thy name for ever and ever.

2 Every day will I bless thee; and I will praise
thy name for ever and ever.

3 Great is the Lord, and greatly to be praised;
and his greatness is unsearchable.

4 One generation shall praise thy works to
another, and shall declare thy mighty acts.

5 I will speak of the glorious honour of thy majesty, and of thy wondrous works.

6 And men shall speak of the might of thy terrible acts: and I will declare thy greatness.

7 They shall abundantly utter the memory of thy great goodness, and shall sing of thy righteousness.

8 The Lord is gracious, and full of compassion; slow to anger, and of great mercy.

9 The Lord is good to all: and his tender mercies are over all his works.

10 All thy works shall praise thee, O Lord; and thy saints shall bless thee.

11 They shall speak of the glory of thy kingdom, and talk of thy power;

12 To make known to the sons of men his mighty acts, and the glorious majesty of his kingdom.

13 Thy kingdom is an everlasting kingdom, and thy dominion endureth throughout all generations.

14 The Lord upholdeth all that fall, and raiseth up all those that be bowed down.

15 The eyes of all wait upon thee; and thou givest them their meat in due season.

16 Thou openest thine hand, and satisfiest the desire of every living thing.

17 The Lord is righteous in all his ways, and holy in all his works.

18 The Lord is nigh unto all them that call upon him, to all that call upon him in truth.

19 He will fulfil the desire of them that fear him: he also will hear their cry, and will save them.

20 The Lord preserveth all them that love him: but all the wicked will he destroy.

21 My mouth shall speak the praise of the Lord: and let all flesh bless his holy name for ever and ever.

146 Praise ye the Lord. Praise the Lord, O
my soul.

2 While I live will I praise the Lord: I will sing
praises unto my God while I have any being.

3 Put not your trust in princes, nor in the son
of man, in whom there is no help.

4 His breath goeth forth, he returneth to his
earth; in that very day his thoughts perish.

5 Happy is he that hath the God of Jacob for
his help, whose hope is in the Lord his God:

6 Which made heaven, and earth, the sea,
and all that therein is: which keepeth truth
for ever:

7 Which executeth judgment for the
oppressed: which giveth food to the hungry.
The Lord looseth the prisoners:

8 The Lord openeth the eyes of the blind:
the Lord raiseth them that are bowed down:
the Lord loveth the righteous:

9 The Lord preserveth the strangers; he relieveth the fatherless and widow: but the way of the wicked he turneth upside down.

10 The Lord shall reign forever, even thy God, O Zion, unto all generations. Praise ye the Lord.

Riches AI misses and cannot provide, to the Rich man who gains riches with his devices

James 3:13 Kjv Who is a wise man and endued with knowledge among you? let him shew out of a good conversation his works with meekness of wisdom.

James 4:16 Kjv But now ye rejoice in your boastings: all such rejoicing is evil.

James 4:4 Kjv Ye adulterers and adulteresses, know ye not that the friendship of the world is enmity with God? whosoever therefore will be a friend of the world is the enemy of God.

James 5:2 Kjv Your riches are corrupted, and your garments are motheaten.

James 5:3 Kjv Your gold and silver is cankered; and the rust of them shall be a witness against you, and shall eat your flesh as it were fire. Ye have heaped treasure together for the last days.

Matthew 6:20-22 Kjv 20 But lay up for yourselves treasures in heaven, where neither moth nor rust doth corrupt, and where thieves do not break through nor steal:

21 For where your treasure is, there will your heart be also.

22 The light of the body is the eye: if therefore thine eye be single, thy whole body shall be full of light.

James 5:3 Kjv 3 Your gold and silver is cankered; and the rust of them shall be a witness against you, and shall eat your flesh as it were fire. Ye have heaped treasure together for the last days.

2 Corinthians 10:5 Kjv Casting down imaginations, and every high thing that exalteth itself against the knowledge of God,

and bringing into captivity every thought to the obedience of Christ.

Matthew 22:36-40 Kjv 36 Master, which is
the great commandment in the law?

37 Jesus said unto him, Thou shalt love the
Lord thy God with all thy heart, and with all
thy soul, and with all thy mind.

38 This is the first and great commandment.

39 And the second is like unto it, Thou shalt
love thy neighbour as thyself.

40 On these two commandments hang all the
law and the prophets.

Psalm 29:3-9 Kjv 3 The voice of the Lord is
upon the waters: the God of glory
thundereth: the Lord is upon many waters.

4 The voice of the Lord is powerful; the voice
of the Lord is full of majesty.

5 The voice of the Lord breaketh the cedars;
yea, the Lord breaketh the cedars of
Lebanon.

6 He maketh them also to skip like a calf; Lebanon and Sirion like a young unicorn.

7 The voice of the Lord divideth the flames of fire.

8 The voice of the Lord shaketh the wilderness; the Lord shaketh the wilderness of Kadesh.

9 The voice of the Lord maketh the hinds to calve, and discovereth the forests: and in his temple doth every one speak of his glory.

Isaiah 14:12 Kjv How art thou fallen from heaven, O Lucifer, son of the morning! how art thou cut down to the ground, which didst weaken the nations!

Revelation 12:7-12 Kjv 7 And there was war in heaven: Michael and his angels fought against the dragon; and the dragon fought and his angels,

8 And prevailed not; neither was their place found any more in heaven.

9 And the great dragon was cast out, that old serpent, called the Devil, and Satan, which

deceiveth the whole world: he was cast out into the earth, and his angels were cast out with him.

10 And I heard a loud voice saying in heaven,
Now is come salvation, and strength, and the kingdom of our God, and the power of his Christ: for the accuser of our brethren is cast down, which accused them before our God day and night.

11 And they overcame him by the blood of the
Lamb, and by the word of their testimony; and they loved not their lives unto the death.

12 Therefore rejoice, ye heavens, and ye that
dwell in them. Woe to the inhibiters of the earth and of the sea! for the devil is come down unto you, having great wrath, because he knoweth that he hath but a short time.

1 John 3:8 Kjv For this purpose the Son of God was manifested, that he might destroy the works of the devil.

Luke 19:10 Kjv For the Son of man is come to seek and to save that which was lost.

John 3:16 Kjv [16] For God so loved the world, that he gave his only begotten Son, that whosoever believeth in him should not perish, but have everlasting life.

www.ingramcontent.com/pod-product-compliance
Lightning Source LLC
LaVergne TN
LVHW052252200926
848481LV00002B/348